CAMBRIDGE
UNIVERSITY PRESS

CAMBRIDGE
Primary English

Learner's Book 5

Sally Burt & Debbie Ridgard

CAMBRIDGE
UNIVERSITY PRESS

University Printing House, Cambridge CB2 8BS, United Kingdom

One Liberty Plaza, 20th Floor, New York, NY 10006, USA

477 Williamstown Road, Port Melbourne, VIC 3207, Australia

314–321, 3rd Floor, Plot 3, Splendor Forum, Jasola District Centre,
New Delhi – 110025, India

103 Penang Road, #05–06/07, Visioncrest Commercial, Singapore 238467

Cambridge University Press is part of the University of Cambridge.

It furthers the University's mission by disseminating knowledge in the pursuit of
education, learning and research at the highest international levels of excellence.

www.cambridge.org
Information on this title: www.cambridge.org/9781108760065

© Cambridge University Press 2021

First published 2015

Second edition 2021

20 19 18 17 16 15 14 13 12 11 10 9 8 7 6 5 4 3 2 1

Printed in Malaysia by Vivar Printing

A catalogue record for this publication is available from the British Library.

ISBN 978-1-108-76006-5 Paperback with Digital Access (1 Year)
ISBN 978-1-108-96425-8 Digital Learner's Book (1 Year)
ISBN 978-1-108-96426-5 eBook

....

Introduction

Welcome to Stage 5 of Cambridge Primary English. Language is your route to a world of knowledge, fun and communication. Language helps you grow and learn, and connects you to every area of life.

We have included exciting fiction texts covering timeless tales and fables from all over the world. We have also included fascinating non-fiction texts that will take you to space and back, and show you how things work.

You will read and produce all kinds of stories, plays, poetry, articles, advertisements, biographies, experiments, film reviews, letters and more, learning to be creative, descriptive, factual and persuasive.

You will do interesting activities in a variety of ways – on your own, in pairs and in groups – to practise reading, writing, speaking and listening for different audiences and in different contexts.

We have included something for everyone:

- Are you good at presenting or interviewing?
- Do you like to research a topic or do you prefer reading fantasy?
- Do you enjoy writing poems or biographies?
- How do you feel about performing?
- Are you better at reading aloud?

This book has all the tools you need to succeed and is full of opportunities for things that interest you and things you enjoy or want to learn to do better. There is also time for reflection, review and feedback so you can understand how to improve.

The book contains a handy toolkit at the end so you can remind yourself of essential language tips and tricks. It also has some spelling practice, showing that spelling can be fun as well as challenging.

We hope you enjoy your journey to language success.

Sally Burt & Debbie Ridgard

Contents

Speaking/Listening	Language focus	Vocabulary	Cross-curricular links	21st – century skills
Read aloud and discuss a fable Discuss animal stereotypes Retell a story from another point of view Listen to information on proverbs Give a presentation on a summary of the fable Give a presentation on a different story ending	Modal verbs Narrative and pronouns Possessive pronouns and adjectives Punctuating dialogue	Words to describe features of fables Shades of meaning verbs Words to describe different personalities and stereotypes Proverbs Synonyms for *said* Literal and figurative language Exploring alliteration Story stage language	History – Ancient Greek storytelling, different sources Science – ants and grasshoppers, making predictions Geography – reference books and maps on Philippines, and coconuts as a crop	Collaboration Active learning
Listen to an interview Ask open and closed questions Role play an interview Have a discussion	Simple and compound sentences Adverbs and adverbial phrases Biography and autobiography features Adverbial clauses Past tense	Words in context Informal words and colloquial speech Specialised 'space' terms Synonyms Skim and scan Viewpoint	History and geography – space exploration, biographies, fact files	Skills for life Creative thinking
Read aloud with expression	Similes Metaphors Personification	Comparisons Figurative expressions Literal and figurative	Geography – gem stones, the sea, weather History – significant poets	Language awareness
Make predictions Listen about classic literature Role play a conversation Read a story aloud using storytelling techniques	Standard English Direct and indirect speech Classifying nouns Quantifiers	Literal and figurative language Character-profile vocabulary Old-fashioned language Language describing register Screenplay language Classic-tale features Classifying nouns Spelling patterns for plurals	Geography – books about India, wild animals and the jungle; books about Greece; books about wild animals and the bush in Africa, Zimbabwe History – Ancient Greece; myths and legends from different cultures	Role play Metacognition
Demonstrate instructions Listen to an interview Listen to a personal account	Style and purpose Simple and compound sentences Connectives Complex sentences	Non-fiction Topic sentence Instructions Explanations Summarise	Science – experiments, salt, crystals Geography – caves	Metacognition Cross-curricular learning
Perform a poem in a group Describe mood and techniques to compare poems	Develop your poetic language Similes, metaphors and personification recap	Types of rhyme Poetic-technique vocabulary Literal and figurative description Figures of speech	Geography – woodland environment; Africa and African plains, drought Science – animals and plants in poem; hedgehogs	Group work Performance Differentiation

Contents

Speaking/Listening	Language focus	Vocabulary	Cross-curricular links	21st – century skills
Retell a story in your own words Summarise a fairy or traditional tale Listen to a *Cinderella* synopsis Present a short, oral report Give a group presentation on how the story ends Listen to how to modernise or adapt a familiar tale Read your tale aloud	Phrases and clauses Two forms of present tense Homophones and homonyms	Fairy/traditional tale features Words to add local colour Story-stages language Synonyms for adjectives Homophones and homonyms Ambiguity Traditional beginnings	Science – salt Geography – books and maps on Iran; books and maps on Kenya and China History – of Iran/Persia, Kenya and China Culture – cultural context of Iran, Kenya and China Geography and culture – of local area Science – plants and fruits including blackberries	Making predictions Collaboration Assessment for learning
Role play a persuasive conversation Give directions Present an oral review	Persuasive texts Adjectives of comparison Style, tone and register	Facts and opinions Persuasive techniques Formal and informal language Register	Geography – holiday destinations, maps Technology – sending emails Environmental awareness	Cross-curricular learning Language awareness
Learn how to write production notes Read aloud with expression Perform a script	Play script and film script features	Story summary Plays and films Genre Version Camera shots and angles Point of view	Geography – Middle Eastern countries and Asia History – ancient cultures Music – to fit the setting and characters	Skills for life Collaboration

How to use this book

In this book you will find lots of different features to help your learning.

What you will learn in
the unit.

We are going to ...

- explore animal stereotypes, discuss story structure and develop ideas about characters.

Questions to find out what
you know already.

Getting started

1 Have you ever heard more than one version of a story?
2 What sort of story was it?
3 Why do you think there was more than one version?

Fun activities
linked to what you
are learning.

3 Ant and Grasshopper approach life differently.
  a Make notes about how each character approaches life.
  b Summarise your ideas to your partner and discuss whether you agree.
  c Sort these adjectives into two lists to describe Ant and Grasshopper.

Important words
to learn.

Key words

folklore: traditional stories and culture of a group of people

moral: something you learn from a story or event about how to behave

Audio recordings of texts and
listening activities.

Key language and grammar
rules explained.

Language focus

Standard English is used in formal narrative writing, although standard English rules can be broken in dialogue. In standard English:

- subjects must agree with verbs
- sentences need correct punctuation according to sentence type: statement, question or command
- capital letters are used at the beginning of a sentence, at the start of dialogue and for proper nouns and adjectives
- apostrophes must be correctly placed to show possession for singular and plural nouns or contractions.

Questions to help you think about how you learn.

> Can you explain the features of a fable?
> How could you make your explanation clearer?

Hints to help you with your reading, writing, speaking and listening skills.

Reading tip

When you read each person's part, try to imagine their expression and gestures, even beyond the stage directions.

A good time to pause and find out how your learning is progressing.

How am I doing?

Did you include your activities, thoughts, feelings and opinions in your blog?
Did you listen to the feedback and use it to improve your work?

This is what you have learned in the unit.

Look what I can do!

- ☐ I can identify similes, metaphors and personification in poems.
- ☐ I can identify key features of a haiku.
- ☐ I can use different words for effect.
- ☐ I can plan, write and edit a haiku poem.
- ☐ I can analyse a poem's language and structure.
- ☐ I can practise and perform a poem as a choral reading.

Questions that cover what you have learned in the unit. If you can answer these, you are ready to move on to the next unit.

Check your progress

1   Decide if the following statements are facts or opinions.
    a   Astronauts must be very brave to live in space.
    b   Astronauts can live in space for five months.
2   Write two simple sentences from this compound sentence:
      The astronauts trained so they were ready for the mission.
3   Join these simple sentences to make a compound sentence:

Projects for you to carry out, using what you have learned. You might make something or solve a problem.

Projects

Group project: choose a cycle, like spring, summer, autumn, winter, or an egg, a caterpillar, a cocoon, a butterfly, and write a haiku to reflect each stage of the cycle. Illustrate and present your poems.

Pair project: draw up a table of figurative language techniques, such as metaphors or alliteration, and give an explanation of each with an example.

Solo project: using poetry anthologies or the internet, choose a haiku and use it to explain the rules for how to write a haiku. Present it as an annotated diagram using the haiku as the example.

1 ▶ There's a lesson in that

⟩ 1.1 Read a story by Aesop

We are going to ...

- read and discuss a fable, and explore features of fables.

Getting started

1 What is a fable? Is it fiction or non-fiction?

2 Discuss what makes the story a fable with a partner.

3 Do you know any of these famous fables: *The Fox and the Crow, The Tortoise and the Hare* or *The Lion and the Mouse*? Tell them to each other or discuss what they may be about.

1   *The Ant and the Grasshopper* is one of Aesop's most famous fables.

   a   Skim read the story silently to get the main idea.

   b   Read the story aloud in your group, one paragraph each.

   •   Do you understand all the words in your paragraph?

   •   Use expression as you read, so you make the meaning clear.

Aesop lived in Greece in the 6th century BCE. No-one's really sure where he came from, but 'Aesop' comes from the Greek word 'Aethiop', which means Ethiopia, so that may be a clue.

Reading tip

When you don't know what a word means, try these ideas:

•   Break the word into syllables and look for a common root word, prefix or suffix.

•   Re-read the word in context for extra clues.

•   Use a dictionary.

•   Add the word to your wordbook.

The Ant and the Grasshopper

One fine summer's day, deep in a meadow, a grasshopper was bouncing about, chirruping and singing without a care in the world. An ant bustled by, weighed down by the enormous ear of corn she was lugging to her nest. Time and time again, the grasshopper watched the ant scurry back and forth gathering food – insects, flies, grains of wheat – anything she could find, never once stopping to admire the glorious day or relax in the rays.

The grasshopper found this difficult to **fathom** and teased her as she busied by saying, "Take it easy there, Ant! Why are you working so hard? The day is long! Food is plentiful. Come and rest awhile and listen to my latest melody."

"As it happens, Grasshopper, I am storing up food for winter and you should be doing the same. Summer won't last forever, you know!" snapped the ant shaking her head and rolling her eyes as she continued on her industrious way, if anything toiling just a little harder. Grasshopper **guffawed** at the idea of working on such a day and hopped happily off into the sunset, singing and jigging all the way.

And summer *didn't* last. It never does. Winter came, bringing barren **fare** and frosty fields. Grasshopper's song stuck in his throat as he shivered without shelter or **sustenance**, gazing **wistfully** at the ants as they munched **liberally** from their stores of food, shaking their heads at him and offering him nothing.

"How foolish I have been!" he wailed, for only then did Grasshopper understand that he should have made provision for winter as Ant had said.

Glossary

fathom: to understand something by thinking about it hard

guffawed: laughed loudly, especially mocking someone or something

fare: food and drink

sustenance: food

wistfully: slightly sad because you are thinking about something you cannot have

liberally: in large amounts

2 Discuss the story in a group.

a Summarise the main idea of the story in two or three sentences.

b Who are the main characters? How are they different in what they say and do?

c One character learnt something important. What was it?

d Which character do you think behaved the best? Use examples to explain your view.

e Who would you rather be friends with – Ant or Grasshopper?

f Fables are found in many cultures and **folklore** traditions. What have you learnt about fables from the story? Write a Fable Fact File in your notebook.

Use these words to help you:

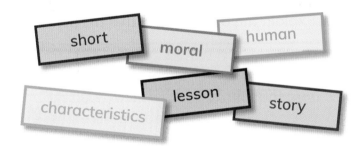

short moral human characteristics lesson story

Key words

folklore: traditional stories and culture of a group of people

moral: something you learn from a story or event about how to behave

FABLE FACT FILE

- Fables are ...
- Usually, the characters ...
- The main point ...
- We can ...

g Discuss other stories you think might be fables.

h Complete your Reading log for *The Ant and the Grasshopper*. Is a story a good way of teaching this lesson? Explain your opinion.

Can you explain the features of a fable?
How could you make your explanation clearer?

> 1.2 Check your understanding

We are going to ...

- explore descriptive verbs and modal verbs

> **Key word**
>
> Modal verb: a verb that expresses possibility, ability, permission or obligation by changing other verbs in a sentence

Getting started

1 Work with a partner and complete a sentence using the verb *must*.

   You must ...

2 Now replace *must* with *may*. Which sentence gives permission, and which one obliges you to do something?

3 Do the same with *could* and *should*. Explain the difference in the effect.

1 Discuss the questions with a partner and then write your answers neatly in your notebook. Use examples from the text.

   a Why did Grasshopper tease Ant?

   b Why did Ant say "Summer won't last forever"?

   c Give an example of Ant's *actions* to show she approves or disapproves of Grasshopper.

   d What made Grasshopper finally understand that he should have acted differently?

   e How do you think Ant felt when she saw Grasshopper at the end?

2   Verbs can tell you about characters through how they act and move.

a   What different kinds of speaking do these words describe?
    Explain the different shades of meaning and use them in role
    plays with a partner. Use a dictionary if you need to.

b   Choose a verb from the story that shows Ant's mood when
    Grasshopper teases her.

c   Write down verbs from the story to describe how Ant moves.
    What do they show about her personality?

d   *Fathom* has more than one meaning in the dictionary.
    Use the context to decide which meaning is correct in the story.

Fathom

– *n.* a unit of measurement (equal to six feet) for water depth

– *v.* to measure the depth of water with a sounding line

– *v.* to understand something by thinking hard about it

   e   What tense is the narrative part of the story? Give three examples.

   f   What tense is the dialogue mainly in? Give three examples.

3   Work with modal verbs.
      Read the Language focus box.

Language focus

Modal verbs express possibility, ability, permission or obligation by changing other verbs in a sentence. Common modal verbs are shown here

Modal verbs are followed by the base verb they change.

*I can <u>dream</u>; you **ought to** <u>eat</u>; she **should** <u>smile</u>.*

Modals can express degrees of possibility – how likely something is to happen:

It could be hot tomorrow.	I may do my homework.
It might be hot tomorrow.	I should do my homework.
It will be hot tomorrow.	I must do my homework.

a   Identify the modal verb and explain the difference between these sentences in terms of how likely they are to happen.

  • The grasshopper might collect food for the winter.

  • The grasshopper will collect food for the winter.

b   Modal verbs can be negative. Identify the modal verbs then turn these sentences into negatives using a contraction.

Example: Ant will collect enough food.
      Ant won't collect enough food.

  • Grasshopper should think about the winter.

  • Grasshopper ought to be more responsible.

  • Grasshopper can spend his time relaxing.

  • Ant must be kind to Grasshopper.

c   Choose a suitable modal verb to complete these sentences.

  • He **chirrups** beautifully.
    He _____ practise a lot.

  • It was so dark in the anthill that Ant _____ see the doorway.

  • Ant is a talented food collector.
    She _____ even carry food balanced on her back.

  • If she collects enough food, she _____ just have enough to last the winter.

  • Grasshopper isn't convinced by hard work.
    He _____ see the point of working in summer.

> **Glossary**
>
> **chirrups:** (especially of a bird) short, high-pitched sounds

> 1.3 Story features

We are going to ...

- explore animal stereotypes, discuss story structure and develop ideas about characters.

Getting started

1 **Anthropomorphism** means giving human characteristics to animals in stories or pictures. *Anthropos* means *man* or *human* in Ancient Greek and *morph* means *shape* or *form*. Can you see how this word came about?

2 Discuss how you think Ant and Grasshopper have been given human characteristics.

1 Animal characters in fables often have particular human characteristics that we associate with each animal. These are known as **stereotypes**.

a Discuss with a partner the characteristics often associated with these animals in stories and films.

Key words

anthropomorphism: giving human characteristics to animals

stereotype: the typical traits associated with a type of character

| rat | bull | hare | dolphin |

| monkey | sheep | bee | tortoise |

b   How does Ant act like a person? Make a list.

c   How does Grasshopper act like a person? Make a list.

d   Read these fact files about real ants and grasshoppers.

   • Which is which?

   • Do the facts match Ant and Grasshopper's personalities? Give your opinion.

A	B
• Live almost anywhere except extremely cold places • Live by themselves • Mostly eat grasses, leaves and cereal crops (herbivore) • Don't usually survive the winter	• Live almost anywhere • Live in colonies • Will eat most things especially insects, meat, fats and sugary foods (omnivore) • Can live from a few months to a few years

e   Write two short paragraphs describing the personalities of Ant and Grasshopper, using examples from the text of how they speak and act.

   Include your idea of what each character thinks of the other based on how they act and their personalities.

2   Stories usually contain an issue or a complication.
   In fables, the issue is the lesson learnt by one of the characters.

a   Discuss the issue in this story.

b   What did either of the main characters do to resolve the problem?

c   How does the story teach us the lesson?

3 Ant and Grasshopper approach life differently.

   a Make notes about how each character approaches life.

   b Summarise your ideas to your partner and discuss whether you agree.

   c Sort these adjectives into two lists to describe Ant and Grasshopper.

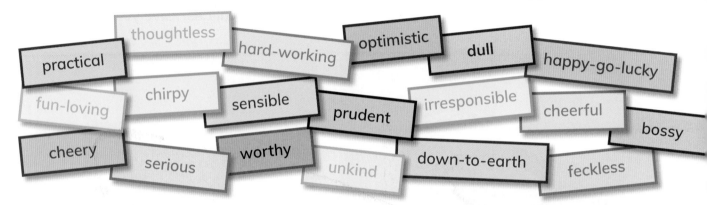

thoughtless   hard-working   optimistic   dull   happy-go-lucky

practical   chirpy   sensible   prudent   irresponsible   cheerful   bossy

fun-loving

cheery   serious   worthy   unkind   down-to-earth   feckless

   d Role play a conversation in which Grasshopper asks Ant for help at the end of the story.

   • What will Grasshopper say?

   • How will Ant react?

   • What could Grasshopper offer Ant in exchange for food?

   e Write a short paragraph explaining what you would say and do if Grasshopper asked you for help. Give reasons.

Glossary

prudent: careful and avoiding risks

worthy: deserving respect, admiration, or support

Speaking tip

Imagine **how** the characters would speak as well as **what** they might say.

How are we doing?

- Exchange your paragraph with a partner.
- Do you agree with your partner's view?
- Have clear reasons been given?

What do you prefer to write with? A pen, a pencil or a computer?

> 1.4 What about my point of view?

We are going to ...

- explore narrative voice, tell a story from another point of view and work with pronouns.

Getting started

How could you make this flow better?

Ant collected Ant's food to have for Ant's supper. Ant decided Ant had the right ingredients for Ant's favourite food.

1 The narrator of a story can either be a character (first person) or someone looking in from outside (third person).

Writing tip

Pronouns stand in for people or objects to avoid repetition.

Example: *The duck said that the duck gave the duck's mum a present.*
The duck said that she gave her mum a present.

a Who tells the story of The Ant and the Grasshopper?

b What evidence tells you this – the narrative or the dialogue? Why?

Language focus

Third-person narrative: an outsider tells the story but is not part of it.

> Imran went to school early so that he could hand in his newspapers for recycling.

First-person narrative: a character tells the story as well as being in it.

> I go to school early so that I can hand in my newspapers for recycling.

Common pronouns: *he, she, it, they, him, her, them, his, hers, theirs*

Common pronouns: *I, we, me, us, mine, ours*

c Which words show whether these sentences are in first or third person?

- Grasshopper said he hoped winter would not come.
- I am worried that Grasshopper will have no food.
- She works so hard and never has time for play.
- We share all the food we collected to see us through winter.
- The ants know they need to store food to survive.

2 Use possessive pronouns and adjectives.

Language focus

Possessive pronouns and **possessive adjectives** do different jobs.

Possessive adjectives appear with the noun they modify.

Possessive pronouns take the place of a noun.

That's **my** <u>book</u>, not **your** <u>book</u>. → That <u>book</u> is **mine**, not **yours**.

possessive adjective   possessive pronoun

Personal pronouns	Possessive adjectives	Possessive pronouns
I	my	mine
you	your	yours
he	his	his
she	her	hers
it	its	–
we	our	ours
they	their	theirs

a   Choose the correct word for these sentences.

- Mimi strapped *(her / hers)* school bag on *(her / hers)* back.
- We paid for the tickets, so they are *(our / ours)*.
- *(Your / Yours)* voice is the loudest in the class.
- Both teams thought the trophy should be *(their / theirs)*.
- Please give back *(my / mine)* jacket.

b   Replace the personal pronoun *(I, you, he/she/it, we, they)* with the correct possessive adjective or pronoun.

- Winter made *(it)* presence felt.
- We are collecting food for *(we)* stores.
- All the food I have collected should be *(I)*.
- They gave me *(they)* word.
- All that I have is *(you)*.

3   Not everyone sees things the same way.
How might the story change if Ant or Grasshopper was telling it?

One fine summer's day, deep in a meadow, I was bouncing about, chirruping and singing without a care in the world …

One fine summer's day, deep in a meadow, I noticed a grasshopper bouncing about, chirruping and singing without a care in the world …

a   Decide with a partner who will tell the story from Ant's and Grasshopper's points of view.

b   Re-read the story and decide what to change to make your character the narrator. You can also change some story details.

c   What does Ant really think about Grasshopper?

d   What does Grasshopper really think about Ant?

e   Make notes of your changes.

f   Tell each other the story from your character's point of view.

Speaking tip

Bring out your character's personality by using informal expressions and words that show what they are thinking.

> 1.5 Proverbs tell a tale

We are going to ...

• explore proverbs, literal and figurative language, and design a cartoon strip.

Getting started

Listen to the information telling you about proverbs and then discuss the following questions.

1   What is a proverb?

2   How do we learn from a proverb?

3   How is a proverb like a fable?

4   What lesson do the four proverbs teach? Discuss how they might be relevant to your life.

Key words

literal: precise; meaning exactly what is said, not exaggerated

figurative: not exact; using imaginative or exaggerated description

1   Stories can help us to learn tricky lessons about life; we remember the story, so we remember the lesson.

a   In a small group, read the following proverbs and explain to each other what they mean.

- Never put off until tomorrow what you can do today.

- All that glitters is not gold.

- Beauty is in the eye of the beholder.

b   **Make hay while the sun shines** is a figurative expression.
Use the cartoon strip to help you discuss what it means literally and then work out the lesson that it teaches.

Reading tip

A dictionary gives you the literal meaning of a word. Figurative descriptions use images to express meaning. We **infer** the meaning from the images.

Key word

infer: work out using prior knowledge

c   Which of the proverbs at the beginning of this activity has the same meaning as *Make hay while the sun shines*?

2   Explain the apostrophe.

   a   Write two uses for the apostrophe, giving an example of each.

   b   Explain the purpose of the two apostrophes in the cartoon strip in Activity 1.

   c   Explain the reason for the apostrophe in these examples from *The Ant and the Grasshopper*.

   • One fine summer's day …

   • Summer won't last forever …

   • And summer didn't last …

   • The grasshopper's song stuck in his throat …

   d   Write two sentences using apostrophes accurately for each of the purposes you identified.

3   Design a cartoon strip to illustrate a proverb.

   a   Choose one of the proverbs from Activity 1. Tell each other an idea for a scenario that could teach the lesson in the proverb.

   b   Plan a cartoon strip of your scenario. Sketch the scene and write dialogue in the speech bubbles.

   c   Add any necessary narrative text. Keep it brief.

   d   Complete the cartoon strip and share it with the class.

> 1.6 A twist in the traditional tale

We are going to ...

- explore a modern version of a fable, make notes of the main points and present a summary of the story.

Getting started

1   Have you ever heard more than one version of a story?

2   What sort of story was it?

3   Why do you think there was more than one version?

1   Explore a modern version of the fable.

   a   Look at another version of *The Ant and the Grasshopper* at the end of this activity, titled *Auntie Anthea and Gentle Geoffrey*. Which is the Ant and which is the Grasshopper? How can you tell?

   b   Predict how this modern retelling (from the title and the pictures) might be similar to or different from the traditional version.

   c   Skim read the story to identify the narrator: is it Geoffrey, Anthea or a third-person narrator?

   d   Read the story together in groups of three. Make notes to summarise the main points. List similarities and differences between this and the traditional version.

Auntie Anthea and Gentle Geoffrey

Summer had been a blast and Gentle Geoffrey had loved every minute. He felt so inspired and his music was sweeter than ever. Auntie Anthea had also enjoyed the summer. Gentle Geoffrey's music had certainly made cleaning and collecting food seem much less effort.

As the weather cooled, Gentle Geoffrey's chirruping became a little less cheerful. Auntie Anthea, on the other hand, was still scrubbing and storing, although it seemed a little more of a chore.

By the time the winter chill set in, Geoffrey felt **famished** and frail. He'd played music all summer with his head in the clouds, so he had no home to go to and no food to eat. But just as he thought he should do something, he caught a faint melody in the whistling wind and once more could think of little else. Auntie Anthea, meanwhile, was warm and well-fed but was finding winter dull, with little to liven up her diet and daily chores. All of a sudden, she thought of Geoffrey.

"What a tasty treat!" she clapped.

"I adore insects and Geoffrey will make a delicious difference. He never knows what's what with all that music swirling in his head. He'll leap at the chance of filling his tummy and I've never grazed on a grasshopper before."

"A … A … Auntie Anthea," shivered Geoffrey, surprised to see her braving the frosty fields. "Wh … wh … whaddya you doing here?"

"I couldn't help thinking of you turning into a block of ice out here," said Anthea, trying to keep the anticipation in her voice **at bay**. "I want a **tenant**, and who could be more delicious, I mean delightful, than you?"

"D … d … delicious? That doesn't sound so c … c … cool. I think I'll g … g … give it a miss, if it's all the s … s … same to you," **quavered** Geoffrey.

"Well, it's not – my heart's set on taking you home for supper," **lured** Anthea. "Just come on inside for a bit."

"A b … b … bit of what?"

"A bit of a bite, of course!" snapped Anthea, with a touch of irritation.

"But a b … b … bite of wh … wh … what?" Geoffrey worried as he crumpled to the ground, too weak to stand.

Anthea dashed forward, slung Geoffrey onto her back, hauled him home and laid him in front of the fire, licking her lips. Geoffrey, revived by the warmth, thought for a moment and then smiled winningly at Anthea.

"Auntie, the other insects said you were, well, mean, but you seem so kind. What can I, you know, do, um, to thank you for your hospitality?"

"Well, I had thought …" Anthea trailed off, hoping her tummy wasn't rumbling too obviously.

"Hmmm! I'd rather sing for my supper than be your supper," Geoffrey declared, and he began to sing, softly at first but gaining in strength with every note. Anthea loved it and suddenly realised what was really good about having Gentle Geoffrey in her home. She could cook and clean and he could keep her company and entertain her friends. Now that would be a giant leap forward for antkind!

Glossary

famished: extremely hungry

at bay: away

tenant: someone who pays rent to use land or live in a building

quavered: shook, usually with emotion or uncertainty

lured: persuaded someone to do something by offering them something exciting

The name Geoffrey has English, French and German origins. It means 'peace'. Do you think it was a good name for the grasshopper in this story?

2 Prepare a short group presentation summarising this version of the story.

a Use your notes and the following questions to prepare your presentation.

- What are Anthea and Geoffrey like? What are their talents?
- What does Anthea intend for Geoffrey at first?
- What does she say that makes Geoffrey reluctant to go with her?
- What shows that Geoffrey knows what Anthea is planning?
- What do you think of his solution to the problem?
- What is the twist in the tale?
- What lesson does this fable teach?
- Which version of the story do you prefer and why?

b Give your group presentation to the class.

c Answer any questions when you have finished.

d Add *Auntie Anthea and Gentle Geoffrey* to your Reading log. Note down whether you preferred this version of the fable or the original.

How are we doing?

- Did you use evidence to explain your comments?
- Did you explain clearly which version you prefer?
- Did you make sure everyone took part in the discussion?

> 1.7 It's all about dialogue

We are going to ...

- **punctuate direct speech, extend a conversation and do a dramatic reading.**

Getting started

1   With a partner, list as many interesting synonyms for *said* as you can.

2   Suggest a way to each rewrite each synonym using *said* + an adverb.
    Example: *said loudly.*

Language focus

Punctuating dialogue

- Put speech marks before and after the spoken words.
- Capitalise the first word inside the speech marks.
- Use a comma after any words introducing the speech.
- Start a new line when a new person speaks.
- If the narrative indicating who spoke (e.g. she said) comes after the speech, put the comma, exclamation or question mark (never a full stop) before closing the speech marks with no capital letter for the word that follows.

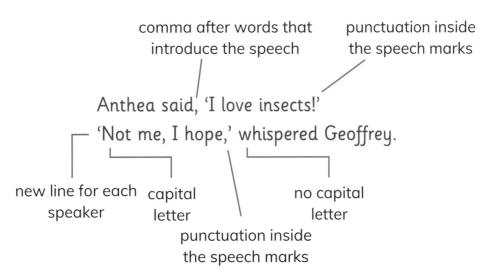

comma after words that introduce the speech

punctuation inside the speech marks

Anthea said, 'I love insects!'

'Not me, I hope,' whispered Geoffrey.

new line for each speaker

capital letter

no capital letter

punctuation inside the speech marks

1 Learn about punctuating direct speech.

    a   Scan the story to locate the punctuation showing dialogue.

- Does it follow the rules in the Language focus box?

- Can you write any other rules to guide you?

    b   Discuss how the punctuation works in the following sentence:

> 'Dearie me,' said Auntie Anthea, 'you look awfully feeble.'

    c   Write these sentences into your notebook, adding the speech marks and correct punctuation, and using interesting verbs to show how the characters speak.

Why would you help me?

Why wouldn't I want to invite you into my house?

Do you really want to help me, or do you want me for another reason?

Now, what on earth could that be?

2 Extend the story.

    a   Continue Geoffrey and Anthea's conversation after Geoffrey finishes singing.

- Write at least two more things for each character.

- Keep the dialogue 'in character'.

- Use the correct punctuation for the dialogue and the narrative.

Writing tip

Try using adverbs to add interest to *said*, *asked* or *replied* instead of replacing them with descriptive verbs.

3 Do a dramatic reading of the dialogue in the story, including your new dialogue.

a Practise reading out just the dialogue with a partner.

b Use the narrative and the way the words are written to help you put across your ideas about the characters. Support your interpretation with speech and gesture.

Speaking tip

You can use an accent as well as words to help your character sound authentic.

Key word

authentic: real, true, genuine or truly representative

What was hard about reading in character?

How could you improve your dramatic reading?

> # 1.8 Figurative language is all around

We are going to ...

- differentiate between literal and figurative language, interpret figurative expressions and explore alliteration.

Getting started

1 Explain the difference between literal and figurative language to a partner.

2 Give an example of a literal and a figurative description of a grasshopper.

1 **Figures of speech** are all around us in our everyday language.

a Discuss these expressions in a small group.

- Do you know these expressions? Talk about what they mean.

- What do they mean literally?

- How might you use them in everyday speech?

Key word

figure of speech: words that are used together in an imaginative way to mean something different from their usual meaning

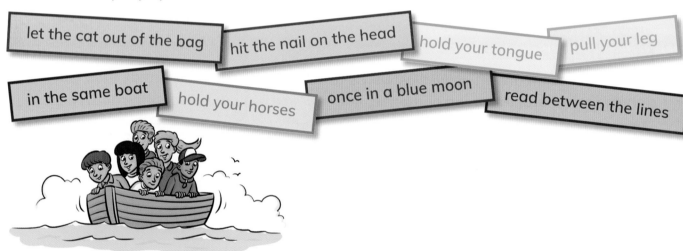

let the cat out of the bag   hit the nail on the head   hold your tongue   pull your leg

in the same boat   hold your horses   once in a blue moon   read between the lines

b Choose three of the expressions and use each one in a sentence.

c Think of some other figurative expressions you know or use.

- In your group, choose one figurative expression each.

- Each draw a literal picture to illustrate your expression.

- Swap your pictures with another group and guess each other's expressions.

d Find the following figurative expressions in *Auntie Anthea and Gentle Geoffrey* in Session 1.6.

- Discuss what they mean literally.

- Discuss what they mean figuratively in the context of the story.

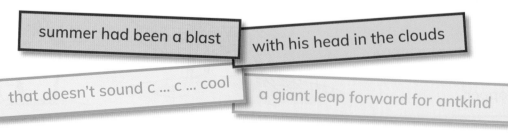

summer had been a blast   with his head in the clouds

that doesn't sound c ... c ... cool   a giant leap forward for antkind

e   In the first version of the fable, Grasshopper's song *stuck in his throat* when winter came. What does this expression mean, both literally and figuratively? How do you think it came about?

f   Geoffrey tells Anthea he would rather **sing** for his supper than **be** her supper. Is he using the expression figuratively or literally? Why?

2   **Alliteration** is a figure of speech because the effect of the repeated consonant sound makes the words more memorable.

> **Key word**
>
> alliteration: use of the same sound or sounds, especially consonants, at the beginning of several close-together words

a   Discuss the effect of alliteration in the names of Auntie Anthea and Gentle Geoffrey.

   • Do the names suit their characters?

   • Invent an alternative name for each character using alliteration.

Super Sipho   funny fatima   Joyful Jacob

b   Think of a word that alliterates with your name and reflects something about you.

c   Anthea often uses alliteration in her speech.

   • Identify three examples of alliteration in her dialogue.

   • How does alliteration make the words stand out?

d   Find three more examples of alliteration in the story. What effect does it have?

> 1.9 Hold a discussion forum

We are going to ...

- **compare fact and opinion, prepare and deliver a group presentation and discuss each other's presentations.**

Getting started

1 What is the difference between fact and opinion?

2 Which is fact and which is opinion?

> The ant collected enough food for winter.

> Grasshopper seems lazy and careless.

3 Share a fact and an opinion about Auntie Anthea and Gentle Geoffrey with the class.

1 Fables are part of the oral tradition; the same story often has different versions, characters, details or endings.

  a In groups of four, discuss an alternative ending to one of the versions of *The Ant and the Grasshopper* fable.

  b Prepare a group presentation to include:

  - which fable you have chosen
  - your thoughts on the discussion points given in the table on the next page
  - an alternative ending to the fable
  - the lesson to be learnt from your alternative ending.

The original version:	The modern version:
• What happened to Grasshopper at the end?	• What happened to Geoffrey at the end?
• What did Ant do about it?	• What did Anthea do when Geoffrey was cold and hungry?
• Do you think this was right?	• Do you think this was right?
• Was Grasshopper lazy?	• Did Geoffrey deserve to be cold and hungry?
• What could Ant or Grasshopper have done to change the outcome?	• What if Anthea had tried to carry out her original plan?
• Explain how the fable could be changed to teach the lesson *A friend in need is a friend indeed*?	• How could the lesson *One good turn deserves another* apply to this fable?

2   Give your presentation.

   a   Give your presentations and discuss each other's ideas.

   b   Listen carefully during each presentation.

      •   Ask questions after each presentation.

      •   Be prepared to offer your ideas but accept others' different ideas as well.

Listening tip

Listen to the complete presentation before deciding what you think about it, otherwise you might miss some of the points.

What was easy and what was hard about giving a clear, interesting presentation?

How could you improve?

> 1.10 Test your knowledge

We are going to ...

•   skim read a story to get the main idea and write a paragraph analysing the features of the story.

Getting started

1   Explain to a partner about standard story structure. What are the different story stages?

2   Use a story you know to show the different story stages.

1   Read the following story from the Philippines independently.

   a   Skim read the story to get the main idea.

   b   Summarise the main idea for yourself in one sentence.

Writing tip

Write multi-clause sentences using connectives to summarise ideas accurately, for example because, but, and so.

The Man with the Coconuts

One day a man who had been to gather his **coconuts** loaded his horse heavily with the fruit. On the way home, he met a boy whom he asked how long it would take to reach the house.

"If you go slowly," said the boy, looking at the load on the horse, "you will arrive very soon; but if you go fast, it will take you all day."

The man could not believe this strange speech, so he hurried his horse. But the coconuts fell off and he had to stop to pick them up. Then he hurried his horse all the more to make up for lost time, but the coconuts fell off again. Many times he did this, and it was night when he reached home.

Mabel Cook Cole

Glossary

coconut: large fruit – like nut with a thick, hard, brown shell covered in fibre, containing a clear liquid and hard, white flesh that can be eaten

2   Use headings to help you summarise a story.

a   Make notes under each heading.

Setting	Characters	Problem	Solution	Ending	Lesson

b   Write a short paragraph explaining whether you would classify *The Man with the Coconuts* as a fable.

- Plan your paragraph carefully, starting with a topic sentence:

  The story can be considered a fable because ...

- Use evidence from the text to support your view.

c   Think of a proverb that would fit the lesson in the story to use in your conclusion.

d   Swap your paragraph with a partner and check it carefully for sense, flow, punctuation, spelling and grammar.

e   Make any changes to finalise your paragraph using your partner's feedback.

How are we doing?

- Can you recognise fable features?

- Can you explain your point of view clearly?

- Can you use evidence from the story to support your views?

> 1.11 and 1.12 Retell a fable

We are going to ...

- **plan, draft and edit a story retelling.**

Getting started

1   Discuss different ways of planning a story with a partner.
    Think of at least three ways.

2   Share ideas as a class and discuss what tools you can use to edit and improve a story.

1   Retelling a familiar story is fun. You don't have to think too hard about the plot because you already know it!

a   Plan a retelling of either *The Ant and the Grasshopper* or *The Man with the Coconuts*. Keep the key features of a fable, but change something, for example:

- choose different characters, names or a different setting
- write a different ending
- use the same characters but teach a different lesson.

b   Use a planning diagram to make notes.

Features of a fable

Short, simple story ✓

Usually animal characters who act like humans ✓

Dialogue shows their characteristics ✓

Figurative language or alliteration ✓

Character learns a lesson ✓

We can also learn a lesson ✓

Section 1: Characters and setting	Section 2: Problem/Issue	Section 3: How the issue works out	Section 4: Lesson to be learnt

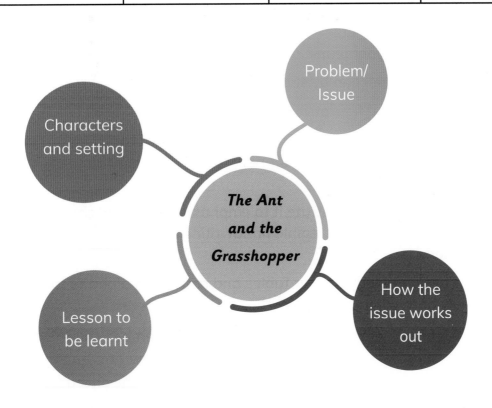

Word wheel for synonyms

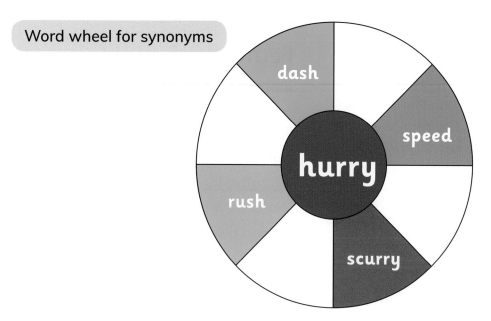

c   Swap plans with a partner.
    Can you tell each other's story aloud, using the plan?

d   Adapt your plan if necessary.

How are we doing?

- Has your partner included the key features of a fable?

- Can you suggest improvements?

2   Write your fable from your plan.

a   Write a first draft, section by section.

b   Include dialogue and figurative language to bring your fable to life.

c   Use the editing checklist in the Toolkit **at the back of this book** to review your work or online. Then ask your partner to read it for flow, sense and originality.

d   Finalise your story and illustrate it to emphasise what has changed from the original. Use neat legible handwriting or use IT for editing and presentation.

e   Make a class anthology of your fables and read them aloud to friends and family or to younger classes.

Remember to start a new line each time a different character starts to speak.

Look what I can do!

- ☐ I can explore the features of a fable.
- ☐ I can identify and use modal verbs.
- ☐ I can compare two versions of a story.
- ☐ I can write dialogue in character using accurate punctuation.
- ☐ I can prepare and deliver a group presentation.
- ☐ I can plan, write and edit a retelling of a fable with my own changes.

Check your progress

1   Name three features of a fable.

2   Identify the modal verb in each sentence:

    a   The man should be more careful with the coconuts.

    b   You could use coconut milk to make a curry.

    c   He must hurry to get there on time.

3   Use each of these modal verbs in sentences of your own.

4   Match these proverbs to their meanings.

Too many cooks spoil the broth.	Have a backup plan. Don't risk all your time, money or effort on one plan.
Birds of a feather flock together.	When too many people try to lead, it's confusing and gives bad results.
Don't put all your eggs in one basket.	People like to spend time with others who are similar to them.

5   Write these sentences in your notebook with the correct direct speech punctuation:

    a   Please help me load these coconuts begged the old man.

    b   She said crossly stop doing that.

    c   Give it to me she snapped because it's mine.

Projects

Group project: research the Philippines, the context for *The Man with the Coconuts*. Find out about the location, size and population; its geographical features, plants and animals; the food, culture, music, language; and things to see and visit. Plan a multimedia presentation on cards, on-screen or as a brochure, or use a mixture of these methods. Include illustrations and photographs, as well as writing. Consider using appropriate props, music or costumes to make your presentation **authentic**. Assign a role to everyone and present your work as creatively as possible.

> ### Glossary
>
> **culture:** the habits, traditions and beliefs of a country, society, or group of people

Pair project: research a fable to role play and present to the class. Adapt the fable where necessary and present with expression and body language to bring it to life.

Solo project: research a fable from your own **culture** or region. Write a summary of the fable, outlining the lesson. Explain how the lesson could apply to our own lives. Give an example.

2 ▶ Exploring space

> 2.1 What is out there?

We are going to ...

- skim a text to get the general idea and scan it for details.

Getting started

1   In pairs, make a list of:
- planets and stars you know about
- space travellers you know about
- facts and words about space you remember.
2   Share this information with the class.

Glossary

catalogue: a list of all the items that exist in one place

astronomer: someone who studies the universe and objects that exist naturally in space

naked eye: ability to see without the help of an instrument

observatory: a building from which scientists can watch the planets, the stars, the weather, etc.

satellite: a natural or artificial object that orbits another object

cosmonaut: a Soviet astronaut

astronaut: a person who has been trained for travelling in space (e.g. members of the NASA space programme)

1 Skim the heading, glossary words and the pictures.

a Can you tell what type of text this is?

A Brief History of Space

In 129 BCE, the first star catalogue was completed by the Greek astronomer Hipparchus.

In 1543, the Polish astronomer Nicolaus Copernicus published his ideas that the Earth revolved around the Sun.

In 1576, Danish man Tycho Brahe, a naked-eye astronomer, built the world's leading observatory in Uraniborg.

In the early 1600s, the first type of telescopes were made by spectacle-makers. They made distant objects appear closer.

In 1609, the Italian scientist Galileo built the first telescope and used his observations to prove Copernicus's theory correct.

In 1704, the English scientist Isaac Newton designed a reflector telescope with greater magnification and a clearer image than earlier telescopes.

In 1926, American Robert Goddard launched the first liquid-fuelled rocket.

In 1946, the idea of a telescope in space was suggested by an American astronomer Lyman Spitzer.

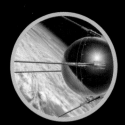

In 1957, the USSR launched the first artificial satellite, Sputnik 1, into space.

On 12 April 1961, Russian cosmonaut Yuri Gagarin became the first person in space. He orbited the Earth in a 108-minute flight.

In 1963, the first woman in space was Russian cosmonaut Valentina Tereshkova.

On 20 July 1969, American astronauts Neil Armstrong and Buzz (Edwin) Aldrin became the first people to walk on the moon.

In 1971, the USSR launched Salyutt 1, the first space station.

In 1983, Sally Ride became the first American woman in space.

Tragically, in 1986, the Space Shuttle Challenger exploded after launch.

In 1991, Helen Sharman became the first British person in space.

In 1995, Valeri Polyakov completed 437 days in space, the longest flight in space so far.

In 2000, the first crew moved into the International Space Station (ISS). It has been occupied ever since.

In 2003, Kalpana Chawla, the first Indian woman in space, died with the crew as the space craft failed when re-entering the atmosphere.

In 2012, Liu Yang became the first Chinese woman in space.

In 2019, Chandrayaan-2 mission: India's first attempt to land on the lunar south pole, which is yet to be explored ...

b   List these words in alphabetical order and then use a thesaurus to find synonyms for them.

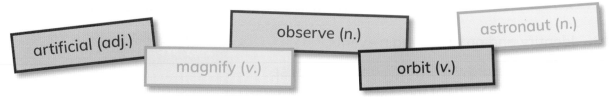

artificial (adj.)   observe (n.)   astronaut (n.)   magnify (v.)   orbit (v.)

c   Use these words in sentences of your own.

d   Add the words to your spelling log.
    Highlight difficult letter groups to remind you.

2 Read the text in Activity 1 aloud and scan it for specific information.

   a Who created the first telescope strong enough to see into space?

   b When was the first human trip into space? What did it achieve?

   c How long ago was the first moon landing?

   d Decide which statement is a fact and which is an opinion.
      Explain the difference.

      • Early astronomers must have had good eyesight.

      • Early astronomers made observations of the stars without a telescope.

   e How many countries are mentioned in this text? Name three of them.

   f Add this explanation text to your reading log.

> 2.2 A simple start

We are going to …

• make notes on a timeline, identify connectives and write multi-clause sentences.

Getting started

Work together in pairs. Use each word in a sentence to describe the features
of the text in Session 2.1.

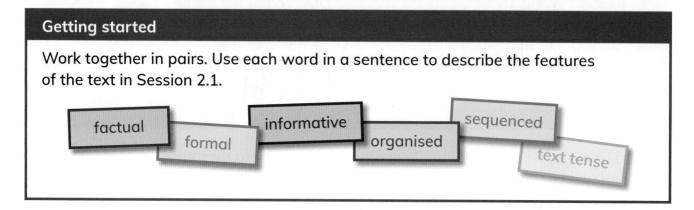

factual   formal   informative   organised   sequenced   text tense

1 Identify and order the main events.

   a In pairs, draw a timeline and summarise
      the main ideas of the text in Session 2.1
      in chronological order. Use dates and key
      words only.

   b Take turns to describe the events to a
      partner using your timeline.

Key words

timeline: a line that shows the
time and the order in which
events have happened

chronological: when events are in
the order in which they occurred

2   Explore simple and compound sentences.

Language focus

A **simple sentence** is the basic building block to writing. A simple sentence:

- always has a subject – who or what is doing the action
- always has a finite verb – action or state of being
- usually has an object – has the action done to it
- deals with one idea.

    Example: The astronauts (subject) entered (verb) the spacecraft (object).

A **compound sentence** is formed by joining two simple sentences with a connective.

    Example: <u>The astronauts entered the spacecraft</u> and <u>they blasted into space</u>.

Common connectives for this job are: *for, and, nor, but, or, yet* and *so*.

A compound sentence is a multi-clause sentence because it has more than one clause.

---

a   In the text *A Brief History of Space* in Session 2.1, identify simple and compound sentences.

- Which type of sentence is used more? Why?

- Give an example of each type.

b   Rewrite these compound sentences.
<u>Underline</u> the verbs and highlight the connectives.

- He invented the telescope, but it was not powerful enough.

- Early astronomers studied the skies for they were fascinated by the stars.

- Scientists invent new rockets so astronauts can go further into space.

- You can become an astronaut or you can become a scientist.

- The satellite is old, yet it is operating well.

- I have never met an astronaut nor have I spoken to one.

Key word

finite verb: a verb that can stand on its own without a helping verb – it has a subject and tense

c Write compound sentences by joining these simple sentences.

Example: Early astronomers observed the moon. They observed the stars too.

Early astronomers observed the moon and they observed the stars too.

- A satellite is a natural object. It is also an artificial object.

- Galileo built a telescope. He could prove Copernicus's theory correct.

- We can fly to the moon. We can't live there yet.

- Astronauts enjoy life on the ISS. They do not stay there for long periods.

- We can visit the museum. We can visit the space centre.

d Write three of your own compound sentences to explain what you've learnt about the history of space.

Writing tip

Use the acronym FANBOYS to remember which connectives help to make a compound sentence.

For And Nor But Or Yet So

FANBOYS

› 2.3 Building language

We are going to ...

- identify and use adverbs and adverbial phrases, and build words with prefixes

Getting started

1 Describe your day so far using the following words:

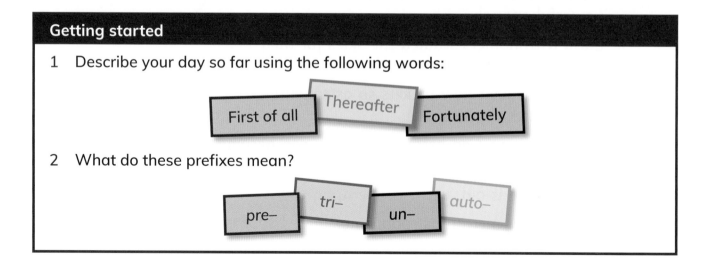

First of all   Thereafter   Fortunately

2 What do these prefixes mean?

pre–   tri–   un–   auto–

1   Find out about adverbs and adverbial phrases.

Language focus

Adverbs are words that describe or modify the verb, adjective or another adverb.

An **adverbial phrase** or **adverbial** is a group of words without a verb that acts as an adverb.

There are different types of adverbials. They add detail and answer the questions:

- time: when?
- place: where?
- manner: how or why?
- quantity: how much?
- quality: to what extent?

a   Work with a partner. Use the text in Session 2.1 to find examples of adverbials of time.

b   Use your timeline from Session 2.2 to write five of your own sentences in chronological order. Use adverbials of time like:

long before   for the first time   eventually   many years later   in 1969   finally

c Identify the type of adverbial <u>underlined</u> in these sentences.

- The first star catalogue was completed <u>in 129 BCE</u>.
- Isaac Newton invented a telescope <u>more powerful than the rest</u>.
- <u>At last</u>, the ISS was ready.
- The first astronauts landed <u>on the moon</u>.
- <u>With great effort</u>, they succeeded.

d Write two of your own sentences using adverbials of place and manner.

2 Work out what these prefixes mean.

a In groups, work out the meanings of these prefixes:

Writing tip

You can start or end your sentences with an adverb or an adverbial phrase.

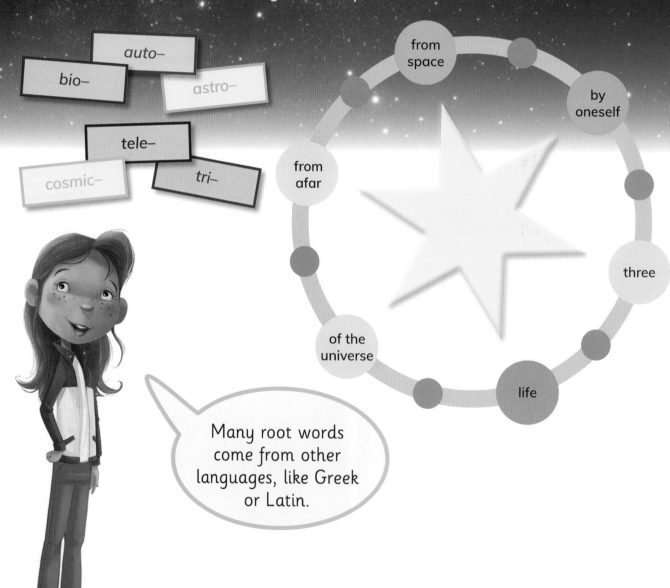

auto–

bio–

astro–

tele–

cosmic–

tri–

from space

by oneself

from afar

three

of the universe

life

Many root words come from other languages, like Greek or Latin.

b   Based on these meanings, what do you think these words mean?

autobiography   triennial   astrodome   teletext   cosmology

c   Look for other words with these prefixes. Use a dictionary to help you.

d   Use these new words to write sentences showing their meaning in context.

How would using more connectives and adverbials improve your writing?

> 2.4 Then and now

We are going to ...

- **explore a journal-style text, compare journals and identify informal language.**

Key word

journal: a written record of what you have done each day, sometimes including your private thoughts and feelings

Getting started

1   How did people record events or send letters and messages to each other in the past?

2   What other ways of recording events and experiences do we have now?

3   How do you think we will communicate in the future?

Many early astronomers and explorers kept journals to record their discoveries. Galileo's 1610 journal shows his sketches of objects around Jupiter. Later, he realised they were moons!

1 Read aloud Sunita Williams' **blog** about life on the International Space Station (ISS) and answer the questions.

a What period of time does this journal cover?

b Is this journal public or private? How can you tell?

c Is the language formal or informal? Give examples of **colloquial** speech.

d What factual information does it include?

e Does it include personal opinions and thoughts? Give an example.

f What is the main tense?

Key words

blog: a combination of the words web and log; a record of your thoughts that you put on the internet for other people to read

colloquial: informal, conversational speech used to communicate with friends and family

Blog   **About**   **Home**   🔍

06

On the ISS

Well, it has been a busy week on the ISS! The main event was the arrival of the Progress **resupply craft**. The long wait was so worth it. Once the spacecraft was **secured**, we **equalised** the pressure and cracked open the hatch. 'Gorby' (our nickname for the Progress) was overflowing with exciting goodies. Not only did we get fresh food, like apples, tomatoes and oranges (I just love that smell), but also chocolate – lots of it! It's great to eat fresh food again, I automatically feel healthier.

There were cards and gifts from FFF (family, friends and fans) back home. Everyone took a little time to themselves to sit back, read and enjoy the news (though old) from home.

Here's one of our crew, Cosmonaut Fyodor N. Yurchikhin, juggling our fresh cargo! Not much skill required since those oranges just hang in the air!

Other activities this week:

- A routine spacewalk to check things out. It went well with the expert help from our ground team. Well done and thanks to everyone
- Our usual daily exercises of cycling, running and pushing weights. You can't miss one day up here – gotta keep our muscles working or they'll forget what to do!
- We chatted to kids from the International Space School in Scotland. Their questions were great AND they invited me to visit them next summer! How awesome.

And finally, my 'favourite' job of all – it was MY turn to clean the station this week ...

Sunita Williams

Glossary

resupply craft: a spacecraft with no crew that delivers supplies to the space station and removes waste

secured: fixed, firmly fastened and not likely to fall or break

equalised: made equal or became equal

Reading tip

Notice how the writer uses informal personal language to convey feelings and mood. How would you describe this astronaut's mood on the ISS?

Now read these social media posts from astronauts:

Sunita Williams

@Astro_Suni 21 Jul

Saturday morning on the ISS. Clean-up over, now for a weightless workout on the treadmill.

Chris Hadfield

@Cmdr_Hadfield 10 May

Who needs a closet when you can store things on the ceiling!

Tim Peake

@astro_timpeake   15 Jan

My first real spacewalk – what an exhilarating experience!

Sam Cristoforetti

@AstroSamantha   20 May

Another busy day working on science experiments and taking pics of Earth.

Christina H Koch

@Astro_Christina   7 May

Let the cargo ops begin! When resupply crafts arrive we get to work stowing the new gear ...

2   Discuss and compare different forms of communication.

   a   Copy this table and make notes to compare these forms of communication.

journal	letter	blog	phone text

- What is the purpose of each text type?
- Who is it addressed to?
- Is it formal or informal?
- Which one gives a personal opinion or viewpoint?
- Is it a modern form of writing?
- Is it persuasive?
- Does it have facts and opinions?

   b   Update your reading log to show that you have read a blog.

> 2.5 and 2.6 Blogging

We are going to ...

- plan a weekly diary together and use diary notes to write, edit and present a blog.

Getting started

As a class, discuss the following:

1 Have you ever kept a journal or a diary? Was it private?

2 What is the difference between a private and a public journal?

3 Have you read a journal of someone famous?

4 What is 'blogging'?

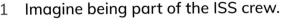

1 Imagine being part of the ISS crew.

a In small groups, discuss the kinds of things you might do as an astronaut on board the ISS. Use the information you have gained so far and add some imagination.

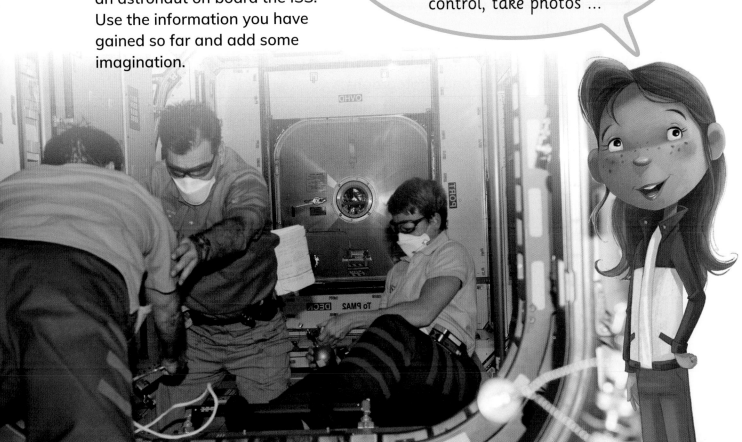

Whew! Astronauts have a lot to do each day ... check food supplies, clean the station, exercise daily for about two hours, update ground control, take photos ...

b Plan a week of activities. Create a timetable or weekly planner and list the activities you might do every day.

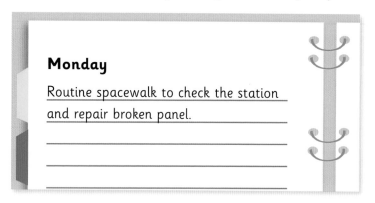

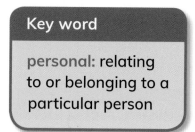

Key word

personal: relating to or belonging to a particular person

2 Write a blog for your family and friends to read.

a Choose one day to write about. Write a paragraph describing the jobs or activities you had to do. Use informal language to describe your personal thoughts, feelings and opinions.

b Share your blog with your group. Help each other check the following:

- You have used friendly, conversational and informal language.

- You have included information and used specialised 'space' vocabulary.

- You have shared your observations, descriptions, personal opinions and reflections.

c Use dictionaries and thesauruses to check your spelling and improve your vocabulary.

d Write your blog neatly. Make it look realistic. You can even add links and photographs.

How am I doing?

Did you include your activities, thoughts, feelings and opinions in your blog?
Did you listen to the feedback and use it to improve your work?

› 2.7 Interviews

We are going to ...

- **listen to an interview, ask open questions and role play an interview.**

Getting started

1 If you met a famous person, what things would you like to know?

2 What questions would you ask?

3 Make a list of rules you think are important when conducting an interview.

1 Listen to an interview with astronaut Chris Cassidy from the ISS and then discuss it.

Listening tip

Listen for the words that are used to ask open and closed questions.

Key words

interviewer: the person who asks the questions during an interview

interviewee: the person who answers the questions during an interview

a Who is the interviewee and who is the interviewer?

b   Are the questions open or closed?
    Give examples to explain your answer.

c   Describe the language used in the
    interview – is the style formal or informal?
    Is the tone serious or friendly?

d   Explain the context of this interview.
    Comment on how and why it is different
    from a normal interview. Are the rules for
    interviews any different?

e   Write three open questions of your own that
    you would like to ask about life on the ISS.

> **Key words**
>
> **closed question:** a question that can be answered with yes or no: Do you enjoy being an astronaut?
>
> **open question:** a question that requires a detailed answer: What do you enjoy about being an astronaut?

2   Role play an interview.

a   Work with a partner. For your interview, choose someone you
    have learnt about in this unit or someone you know personally.

b   Write five questions you would like this person to answer,
    then prepare the answers.

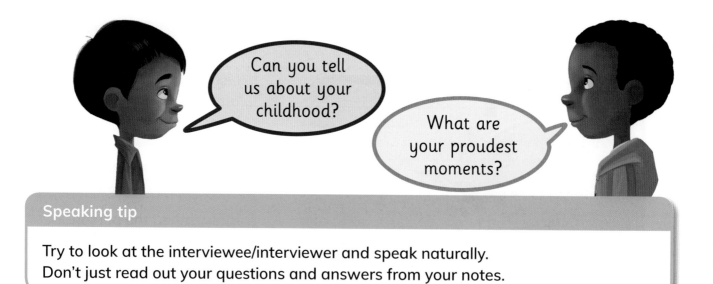

Can you tell us about your childhood?

What are your proudest moments?

Speaking tip

Try to look at the interviewee/interviewer and speak naturally.
Don't just read out your questions and answers from your notes.

c   In pairs, role play the interview. Take turns to interview each other.

d   Present your interview to your group.

How are we doing?

- Did the interviewer ask open questions?
- Did the interviewee give a detailed answer?
- Did both speak clearly? Did they use appropriate register?

Which role do you find more challenging – the interviewer or the interviewee? Which one do you prefer?

> 2.8 Biographies

We are going to ...

- **explore features of a biography and identify the point of view of the writer.**

Getting started

Discuss these questions as a class.

1 What is the difference between a biography and an autobiography?

2 What headings would you like to have in a biography about your life?

1 Identify features of a biography. Skim read the text and discuss the questions.

Astronaut Samantha Cristoforetti
by Year 5 learners, Hillside School

Samantha Cristoforetti is an **ESA** astronaut.

Personal background

She was born in Milan, Italy, on 26 April 1977. In 2015, she set the European record for the longest time in space (200 days) where she celebrated her 38th birthday.

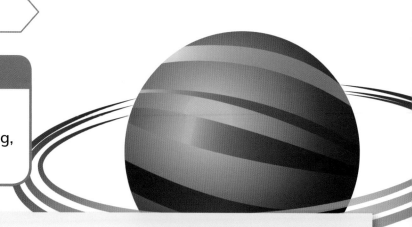

Glossary

ESA: European Space Agency

aeronautics: the science of designing, building, and operating aircraft

Education

In 2001, Samantha graduated with a master's degree in mechanical engineering and then she completed a bachelor's degree in **aeronautics**.

Training

After she graduated, Samantha joined the Italian Air Force and earned her fighter pilot wings. In May 2009, she was selected as an ESA astronaut. Three years later, she was assigned to fly on the Soyuz TMA-15M, as part of the crew of Expedition 42/43 on the ISS.

The Futura Mission

On 23 November 2014, Samantha's dream came true as she launched into space. While on board the ISS, she conducted experiments like keeping worms and insects alive and growing plants. Samantha returned to Earth on 11 June 2015.

Current work

Back on Earth, Samantha works at the European Astronaut Centre, on various projects. She is also part of a team working to improve communications in astronaut operations.

Future plans

Looking ahead, Samantha will continue her training as an astronaut, which will include a mission to the bottom of the Atlantic Ocean. Also, she plans to develop an ESA programme for learners and teachers in schools.

Interests

Samantha enjoys learning foreign languages and her current challenge is Chinese. She likes to read, hike, scuba dive and practise yoga. She enjoys sharing her experiences on Twitter where she has almost a million followers.

Conclusion

Samantha is an inspiration to anyone wanting to follow their dreams. She believes anything is possible. In her own words: 'The sky is not the limit'.

Reading tip

Remember to use the context of a word to work out its meaning. Ask yourself:

How does it fit into the sentence? How does the sentence fit the topic?
What could it mean?

Read a few short social media posts about Samantha's adventures.

ESA 11 Jun
ESA astronaut @AstroSamantha will swap her spacesuit for dive gear this month as commander of a 10-day international research and exploration mission to the Atlantic Ocean floor.

Samantha Cristoforetti 21 Jun
Less than an hour to splash-up ... time to return to the surface and rejoin the 'topsiders'. Looking forward to seeing the sunlight and have a hot shower, but I will miss Aquarius.

NASA_NEEMO 21 Jun
This place @ReefBase is special. Our aquanauts have called it home for a little over a week, living and working underwater so we can learn the best exploration strategies for the moon.

ESA space history 26 Apr
Happy Birthday to ESA's @ AstroSamantha Cristoforetti (26 April)! Samantha spent almost 200 days on @ Space_Station as part of her #Futura mission in 2014–15. She holds the record for the longest uninterrupted spaceflight of a European astronaut.

a Discuss and answer true or false to these statements.
A biography usually:

- is written in sequence
- is organised into sections
- is written mostly in the future tense
- contains facts about a person's life
- uses mostly informal language and vocabulary
- uses first-person narrative (*I, me, we*).

2 Read the text *Astronaut Samantha Cristoforetti* aloud and identify the point of view.

> **Language focus**
>
> | **Biography** | **Autobiography** |
> |---|---|
> | Third-person narrative: Another person gives an account of someone else's life. | First-person narrative: Someone gives a personal account of their own life. |
> | The language may be positive or negative. | The language is likely to be positive. |
> | Common pronouns: *he, she, it, they, him, them, his, hers, theirs* | Common pronouns: *I, we, me, us, mine, ours* |

    a   Who wrote this biography?

    b   Find examples of the use of third-person pronouns in the biography.

    c   Copy these sentences into your notebook. Fill in the blanks with the correct third-person pronouns.

- _____ enjoys her work. Those good results are _____ .

- He loved the experience. The memories are _____ forever.

- The crew knew the spacecraft was _____ because _____ trained in it.

- My friends are going to watch a film about space. I'd love to go with _____ to watch _____ .

- The rocket powered up, then _____ blasted into space and _____ disappeared.

3 Scan the biography for details.

    a   Who is the biography about? Is this person still alive?

    b   When and where was this person born?

    c   Identify three other facts in the text. Are there any opinions?

    d   Why did the writer choose to include mainly facts?

e   Work out the meaning of these words in context: assign, conduct, launch.
    Record the words and any other new words in your spelling log.

f   Who do you think wrote this biography – a fan or an enemy of the person?
    Explain how the point of view of the writer is expressed in this biography.

g   How is this text different to a timeline or a blog?
    Describe the difference in terms of:

h   Add this biography to your reading log.
    List other biographies you would like to read.

> 2.9 Add details

We are going to ...

- revise clauses, and identify and use adverbial clauses in sentences.

Getting started

1   Explain the answers to the following phrases with a partner:

- What is a phrase?

- What is a clause?

2   Give examples to show the difference. Share your ideas with the class.

1 Revise clauses. Read the Language focus box and answer the following questions.

Language focus

A **clause** is a group of words with **a finite verb**. A clause can stand alone as a simple sentence (main clause), or it can join other clauses or phrases to form compound or complex sentences. Some clauses depend on the main clause for meaning (e.g. adverbial clauses).

An **adverbial clause** acts as an adverb. The entire clause modifies the main verb to express *when, where, how, how much* or *under what condition*.

<u>when</u> *they land,* <u>where</u> *it crashed,* <u>as</u> *it begins,* <u>because</u> *she works hard,* <u>although</u> *he tried*

Adverbial clauses come at the beginning or end of a complex sentence.

adverbial clause

The astronaut returned home <u>after she completed the mission</u>.
<u>After she completed the mission</u>, the astronaut returned home.

When the adverbial clause starts the sentence, it is handy to use a comma to help make sense of the sentence.

---

a Decide if the <u>underlined</u> words are adverbial phrases or adverbial clauses.

Example: <u>As a child</u>, she dreamed of going into space. (phrase)

<u>When she was growing up</u>, she dreamed of going into space. (clause)

- He landed the spacecraft <u>the following day</u>.
- <u>As they blasted into space</u>, the astronauts gave a big cheer.
- <u>Without any warning</u>, the rocket exploded.
- They orbited the Earth <u>before they re-entered the Earth's **atmosphere**</u>.
- <u>After three months</u>, the astronauts returned safely to Earth.
- The crowd cheered <u>when the capsule landed</u>.

Glossary

atmosphere: the layer of gases around the Earth

b   Identify the adverbial clause in each sentence. Re-order it and rewrite the sentence. Remember to include a comma when the clause begins a sentence.

Example: He smiled as the rocket launched.
         As the rocket launched, he smiled.

- The spacecraft landed safely after it entered the Earth's atmosphere.
- The crowd cheered as the capsule opened.
- Everyone watched the day they landed on the moon.
- The astronaut completed the mission although he felt sick.
- The space crew were overjoyed when the fresh supplies arrived.

c   Make a list of three adverbial clauses in the *Astronaut Samantha Cristoforetti* biography, in Session 2.8.

2   Improve your writing.

a   Write complex sentences using these adverbial clauses to start or end your sentence.

- after she completed her studies
- although she is young
- when they chose the team
- because she did well
- when she attended school

b   Choose someone in your family or a partner and write five sentences about this person using adverbial clauses and phrases.

c   Use your sentences to write a short biographical introduction about this person.

> 2.10 Tackle tenses

We are going to ...

- identify the tense in a text, practise the simple past tense and form the past tense with the verb to *have*.

Getting started

1 With a partner, complete these statements:

- I was born on ...
- I attend school at ...
- I would like to become ...

2 What tense did you use for each statement?

1 Read the biography of Samantha Cristoforetti in Session 2.8 again, and discuss the tenses used.

a What tense is used in these sections of the biography? Give examples of each.

- Personal background/Education
- **Current** work/Interests
- Future plans

b Which tense is used the most? Why?

c How does the tense fit the purpose of the text?

Glossary

current: happening or existing now

2   Recall the past tense.

Language focus

Regular past tense verbs get –ed	Irregular verbs change
call – called	feel – felt
play – played	fly – flew
stop – stopped	swim – swam
waste – wasted	think – thought

The past tense can also be formed using the verb to have as a helping verb. The helping verb agrees with the subject. (*I have, we have, you have, she has, he has, it has, they have.*)

Example:

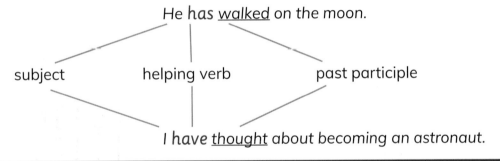

He has <u>walked</u> on the moon.

subject   helping verb   past participle

I have <u>thought</u> about becoming an astronaut.

Writing tip

If a one-syllable word ends in a consonant after a short vowel sound, then double the consonant: drop – *dropped,* slam – *slammed,* plug – *plugged,* rob – *robbed.*

When a word ends with an –e, drop it and add –ed: store – *stored,* use – *used,* bake – *baked.*

Irregular verbs are tricky to spell because they don't follow a rule or a pattern. You just have to memorise them, practise them and recognise them: eat – *ate,* go – *went,* fly – *flew.*

a Change these sentences to the simple past tense. Follow these steps:

- Identify the verb.

- Decide if the verb is regular or irregular.

- Check your spelling and write the sentence in the simple past tense.

Example: She <u>studies</u> astronomy at university. (regular verb)
   She studied astronomy at university.

- He discovers that the Earth moves around the sun.

- He begins a career as an astronomer.

- She becomes famous for her brave work.

- They build an enormous observatory.

- My friend dreams of going into space.

- The astronauts speed towards the moon.

b Write out the sentences using the correct form of the helping verb to *have*.

Example: The astronaut <u>has</u> written a blog in space.

- The astronomer [have] noticed a new star.

- I [has] read a book about space.

- He [have] been in space for six months.

- The satellite [have] launched into space.

c Write out these sentences using the correct verb form to follow the helping verb.

- I have [write] a biography about an astronaut.

- We have [study] all the planets in our solar system.

- Tim Peake has [visit] the International Space Station.

- It has [take] three days to reach the moon.

d Write four sentences in the past tense using the helping verb to *have*.

Example: I have worked …

Do you find changing tense difficult? What can you do to improve?

> 2.11 and 2.12 Write a biography

We are going to …

- use notes to plan a biography, design a layout, proofread and present a biography.

Getting started

1 Make a list of questions you would ask someone if you were planning to write their biography. How would you organise them into different sections?

2 Recall the features of a biography.
   Make a list of things you need to include.

Glossary

ISRO: Indian Space Research Organisation

geo-synchronous: synchronised with or matching the Earth's rotation

1 Read a fact file about a space engineer who works on the ground and then read the social media posts beneath it. Use them to plan her biography.

Fact file

Name:	Anuradha TK
Occupation:	Scientist and satellite project director of the **ISRO**
Born:	1961 in Bangalore, Karnataka
Education:	Bachelor's degree in Electronics
Career:	Works at ISRO satellite centre in the area of **geo-synchronous** satellites

Position:	Heads a team of 20 engineers to develop and launch ISRO satellites into space
Speciality:	Check out systems that observe a satellite's performance once it is in space
Achievements:	First woman project satellite director at ISRO 2019 satellite moon landing to explore moon's south side for the first time ever.
Awards:	2003 Space Gold Medal award by Astronautical Society of India for services in Space sciences
	2011 Suman Sharma Award by National Design and Research Forum (NDRF) of IEI
	2012 ASI-ISRO Merit Award for Realisation of Indigenous Communication spacecraft
	2012 ISRO Team Award 2012 for being team leader for the realisation of GSAT-12

ISRO 1 May

We are ready for one of the most exciting missions, #Chandrayaan2. Launch window between July 9-16 & likely moon landing on Sept 6, 2019. Carrying 3 modules of this #lunarmission – Orbiter, Lander (Vikram), Rover (Pragyan). More updates soon.

ISRO 6 Sep

This is Mission Control Centre. Vikram Lander descent was as planned and normal performance was observed up to an altitude of 2.1 km. Subsequently, communication from Lander to the ground stations was lost. Data is being analysed.

NASA 7 Sep

Space is hard. We commend ISRO's attempt to land their Chandrayaan2 mission on the moon's South Pole. You have inspired us with your journey and look forward to future opportunities to explore our solar system together.

ISRO 7 Sep

Chandrayaan2 mission was a highly complex mission, which represented a significant technological leap compared to the previous missions of ISRO to explore the unexplored South Pole of the moon.

a Choose your own headings and decide how to lay out the information. Is the order important? If possible, do further research to find out about Anuradha's childhood, other interests and family.

b Write a first draft. Use this list to guide you:

- Use your own words and sentences. Include multi-clause sentences and adverbials.

- Use the correct tense for each section. (It should be mainly in the past tense.)

- Use third-person narrative. (*he, she, they*)

2 Edit your work.

a Ask your partner for feedback and ways to improve.

b Check and edit your work. Use the editing checklist in the Toolkit **at the back of this book**. Don't forget to use a dictionary, to correct your spelling, and a thesaurus to improve your vocabulary.

3 Present your biography. Use the checklist to help you.

a Write your biography in neat handwriting or use on-screen tools to type it.

b Include a heading and some pictures.

- neat and organised with headings ☑

- correct tense in each section ☑

- third-person narrative ☑

- simple, compound and complex sentences ☑

- facts and main events in order ☑

Look what I can do!

☐ I can skim and scan a text for information.

☐ I can identify and write multi-clause sentences.

☐ I can identify and use adverbial phrases and clauses.

☐ I can use informal language to write a diary or blog.

☐ I can role play an interview using open questions.

☐ I can write a biography in the correct tense and narrative voice.

Check your progress

1 Decide if the following statements are facts or opinions.

   a Astronauts must be very brave to live in space.

   b Astronauts can live in space for five months.

2 Write two simple sentences from this compound sentence:

   The astronauts trained so they were ready for the mission.

3 Join these simple sentences to make a compound sentence:

   She was the best astronaut. She did not go on the first mission.

4 Write out the adverbial phrase in these sentences:

   a Before noon, they reached the ISS.

   b The capsule landed in the sea.

5 Write out the adverbial clause in these sentences:

   a Everyone cheered when they landed.

   b As they took off, the engines blasted them away.

6 Change these sentences into the past tense:

   a The rocket flies to the moon.

   b We will learn all about space.

Projects

Group project: create a timeline of the history of flight, including space flight. Use your timeline to give a multi-media group presentation, including on-screen video clips and audio.

Pair project: choose a person or an event related to space travel. Create a fact file, including illustrations. Focus on the layout of the fact file to make it quick and easy for someone to read the information.

Solo project: choose someone who has made an impact during their life. Use at least three different sources and make notes on your chosen person, listing underneath where you sourced the information.

Group work can be tricky. What could these roles involve? time-keeper, noise control, deadline manager, general organiser

How are we doing?

Assess other groups' work and give positive feedback and suggestions for improvement.

- Is there a clear timeline?
- Is the information organised?
- How effective is the presentation?

Reading tip

Ask an adult before going online to find information. Make sure you use a reliable source of information. Avoid sites that are out of date or full of advertisements.

3 > Reflections

> 3.1 *Like* and *as*

We are going to ...

- read and explore a poem, identify similes and make comparisons.

Getting started

1 Use these expressions in sentences:

> as hard as rock
>
> as clear as mud
>
> as black as coal
>
> as precious as a jewel

2 Explain the difference between literal and figurative language.

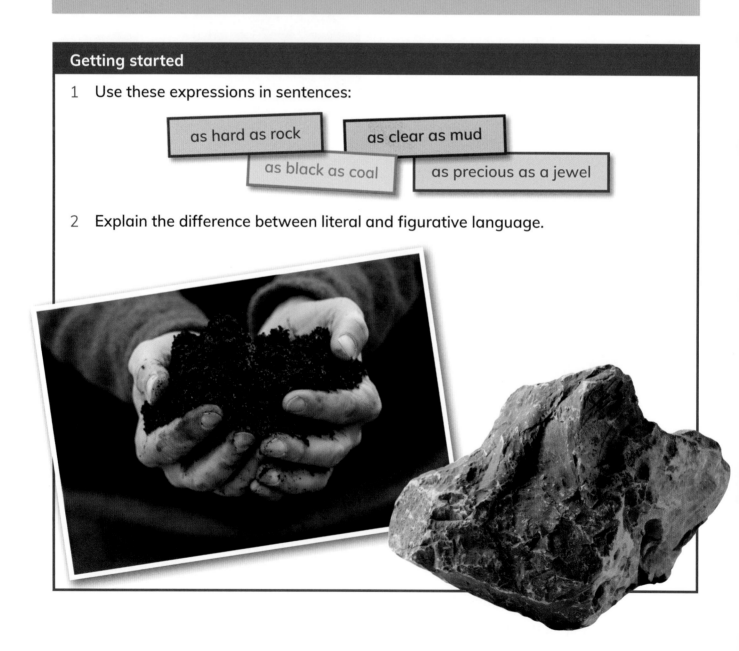

1   Read and discuss a poem by a classic author.

flint

An emerald is as green as grass,
A ruby red as blood;
A sapphire shines *as blue as heaven*;
A **flint** lies in the mud.

A diamond is a brilliant stone,
To catch the world's desire;
An opal holds a fiery spark;
But a flint holds fire.

Christina Rossetti

Glossary

flint: a very hard, grey stone that can be used to produce a flame

Christina Rossetti (1830–94) was educated at home in England by her mother. She dictated her first story to her mother before she could write. She wrote poems and songs for adults and children about love and nature.

Language focus

A **simile** compares things by using the words *like* or *as*.

Examples: *It's **like** an oven in here.*
            *It's **as** hot **as** an oven in here.*

a   In pairs, read the poem silently and then take turns to read it aloud.

Listening tip

Listen for the rhythm of the poem as your partner reads.
Which words does the rhythm emphasise?

b   This poem was written over 100 years ago.
Does this make any difference to its meaning and appeal?

c   What do emeralds, rubies, sapphires, diamonds and opals have in common?

d   Which gemstones are 'as green as grass', 'as red as blood' and
as blue as heaven?

e   Make up other similes. Think of as many as possible.

   • As green as ...

   • As red as ...

   • As blue as ...

f   Why is there no simile for the diamond?
Invent your own simile.

2   Explore the deeper meaning of the poem
in groups.

a   In what way is flint similar to the
other stones?

b   How does the flint **contrast** with the
other stones in the poem:

   • in its appearance?

   • in its usefulness?

c   What does the term *holds fire* mean?

d   Which of these words describe what flint is capable of?

> **Key word**
>
> **contrast:** an obvious difference
> between two people or things;
> a comparison that shows
> how two things are different,
> not similar

energy   power   force   life   strength

e   Explain the message of the poem in your own words.

f   Explain which stone you would rather have with you:

   • at a party

   • in an emergency.

g   Make up two similes to describe flint.

   Examples: as useful as flint, as sparky as flint

> 3.2 Imagine with metaphors

We are going to ...

- explore images in a poem, and identify and write metaphors.

Getting started

Poets are often inspired by nature. Their reactions can be positive or negative.

1   Have you ever been surprised, scared or amazed by something in nature?

2   How do you feel about: the sun, the rain, summer, winter, the dark and sunrise?

1   Read the poem and identify the comparison.

The Sea

The sea is a hungry dog,
Giant and grey.
He rolls on the beach all day.
With his clashing teeth and shaggy jaws
Hour upon hour he gnaws
The rumbling, tumbling stones,
And 'Bones, bones, bones, bones!'
The giant sea-dog moans,
Licking his greasy paws.

And when the night wind roars
And the moon rocks in the stormy cloud,

He bounds to his feet and **snuffs** and sniffs,
Shaking his wet sides over the cliffs,
And howls and hollos long and loud.

But on quiet days in May or June,
When even the grasses on the **dune**
Play no more their reedy tune,
With his head between his paws
He lies on the sandy shores,
So quiet, so quiet, he **scarcely** snores.

James Reeves

79   >

Language focus

A **metaphor** compares two things by saying or suggesting that one thing is another thing.

Example: A diamond is love.

You can change similes to metaphors by removing the words *like* or *as*.

Example: The sea is like a hungry dog.
The sea is a hungry dog.

Glossary

snuffs: breathes noisily

dune: a hill of sand in the desert or by the sea

scarcely: hardly; to do something not very well or very much

a   Listen as your teacher reads the poem. Talk about what you enjoyed.

b   Discuss unfamiliar words in the poem. Use a dictionary to check the meaning and a thesaurus to find synonyms for these words:

shaggy   gnaw   bound   howl   hollo

c   What is the sea compared to? List three things that show this.

d   How does the poet feel about the sea?
Do you agree? How do you feel about the sea?

e   Take turns to read the poem aloud to each other with expression to show the mood.

Reading tip

When you read a poem, the end of a line is not always the end of a sentence. You don't always need to stop at the end of each line.

2   Explore metaphors.

a   How would you compare the following things? Match the descriptions with the pictures that follow and then explain your choice. Add any other ideas you have.

Wildly spinning top   Lonely night traveller   Long, cold fingers

Good friend   Ancient watchtower

The moon

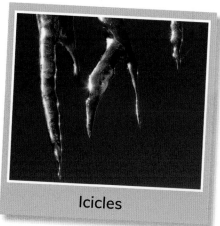

Icicles

A tornado

A large, shady tree

A mountain

b   Imagine other ways to describe the sea using different metaphors.
    Write five sentences that begin with:

    The sea is a ...

c   Rewrite the first three lines of the poem, *The Sea*, in Activity 1
    using a different metaphor.

d   Add this poem to your reading log and comment on the type
    of figurative language used.

Do you like using figurative language?

Could you use it to improve your writing and speech?

〉 3.3 Haiku

We are going to ...

- read and explore the structure of haiku poetry and add to our reading log.

Getting started

1   In small groups, clap the syllables in each of your names.

2   Count the syllables in the following words:

poem   haiku   syllable   figurative   poetry

Key word

syllable: a word or part of a word that has one vowel sound

Haiku is an ancient form of Japanese poetry. In Japanese, there is no plural for *haiku*, so in English we often add other words, such as *poems* or *poetry* to make the plural: *haiku poems*.

1   Read and discuss examples of haiku poetry.

An old silent pond ...
A frog jumps into the pond,
splash! Silence again.

Matsuo Bashō (1644–94)

Toward those short trees
We saw a hawk descending
On a day in spring.

Masaoka Shiki
(1867–1902)

Summer sun gives, takes
Sweetens fruits but scorches earth
All is in balance

Stan Holroyd

Boiling, hot lava
Bubbles beneath the Earth's crust ...
Shhhh! The giant stirs.

Debbie Ridgard

a   Discuss these questions:

What are your first impressions? How would you describe these poems?

How are they similar and how are they different?

b   After your discussion, make up three rules for haiku poetry.
Share them with the class.

Are the lines arranged in stanzas?

Is there a rhyming pattern?

How long are the lines?

How many lines are there?

How is punctuation used?

How many words are there per line?

What is each line about?

How many syllables are there per line?

What is the common **theme** of these haiku poems?

Are they serious or funny?

c   Add the haiku poems from Activity 1 to your reading log. Compare old and new forms of haiku poems and suggest similarities or differences.

2   Analyse the features in detail.

> **Key word**
>
> theme: the unifying idea of a book, story, poem, film or speech

A haiku is traditionally about nature.

The first part describes the *what* and *where* using literal language.

Penguins, black and white
Surviving in icy seas
Stately emperors

The last line is often an interesting or contrasting idea or emotion using figurative language, especially metaphors.

The last word is often, but not always, a noun.

a   A haiku uses a few carefully chosen words to express a feeling without actually naming it. What words in this poem show how the writer feels about penguins?

b   Clap the syllables. Do the words fit the following format?

1-2-3-4-5 syllables

1-2-3-4-5-6-7 syllables

1-2-3-4-5 syllables

Writing tip

A syllable can have more than one vowel or consonant, but only one vowel sound. For example, these words have only one vowel sound: trees (two vowels make one sound), shame (silent e), fly (y acts as a vowel).

The word stately has two syllables and two vowel sounds: the silent 'e' does not count as a syllable: state-ly.

c   Find two synonyms for each word and identify how many syllables each word has.

Example: *cold* (one syllable) *icy* (two syllables) *shivery* (three syllables)

stately   emperor   surviving   seas

d   Change the words in the poem to create your own version. Write it neatly.

Example: The middle line could be: *Playing in icy water* (7 syllables)

> 3.4 Create a haiku

We are going to ...

- make notes, explore vocabulary, then write, edit and present a haiku poem.

Getting started

In groups, make a list of ideas for haiku topics. Use the pictures to inspire you.

A haiku poem is a small poem with a big idea.

1   Make notes (plan to write).

   a   Choose a topic that interests you, surprises you, reminds you of something or makes you feel happy, sad or amazed.

   b   Write a heading and make three columns underneath for making notes.

   - In Column 1, write words that describe your topic literally. What do you see, hear, touch, taste, smell or feel about it?

   - In Column 2, experiment with different words. Use a thesaurus to find new words.

   - In Column 3, write comparisons (particularly metaphors) to describe it in surprising and original ways.

Example notes:

The sea		
Literal words	**Different words**	**Comparisons and metaphors**
large, blue sea	aqua, ocean, expanse	ancient, salty, **sage**

2   Write and edit a first draft.

   a   Read the *How to Haiku* poem, then plan your first draft.

   Remember to be original and express your own feelings, images and ideas.

   b   Swap with a partner and give each other some useful feedback.

   - Read through the poem.

   - Clap the syllables.

   - Give ideas for other interesting words and try them out.

   - Check the metaphor and suggest ways to improve it.

   c   Now edit and rewrite your haiku.

Glossary

sage: wise or wise person

How to Haiku

Name it literally

Add figurative language

Express a key thought

3   Present with impact.

   a   A haiku is small, but it makes a big impact. Present it with impact.

- Use an A4 piece of paper.
- Write the poem in the middle.
- Illustrate it.

   b   Display it with the other haiku poems in the class.

How are we doing?

Read the haiku poems. Answer the questions to assess
your own and each other's haiku poems.

- Is the theme about nature?
- Do the syllables fit the 5-7-5 pattern?
- Is there a literal image or description in the first part?
- Is there figurative language in the last line?
- What is the interesting idea, surprise or contrast in the last line?

> 3.5 Personification in poems

We are going to ...

- read and analyse a poem to identify figurative language and structure.

Getting started

Listen to two poems: *Who Has Seen the Wind?* by Christina Rossetti and
Listen by Telcine Turner.

1   What or who is the wind compared to in each poem?

2   Which poem do you prefer? Why?

3   What is the mood or atmosphere of each poem?

1 Explore the language, mood and structure of a poem by Dionne Brand.

Wind

I pulled a hummingbird out of the sky one day
   but let it go,
I heard a song and carried it with me on my
   cotton **streamers**,
I dropped it on an ocean and lifted up a wave
   with my bare hands,
I made a whole canefield tremble and bend
   as I ran by,
I pushed a soft cloud from here to there,
I hurried a stream along a pebbled path,
I scooped up a yard of dirt and hurled it in the air,
I lifted a straw hat and sent it flying,
I broke a limb from a **guava** tree,
I became a breeze, bored and tired, and hovered and
   hung and rustled and lay where I could.

Dionne Brand

Glossary

streamers: long, narrow pieces of coloured paper used to decorate a room or place for a party

guava: a round yellow tropical fruit with pink or white flesh and hard seeds, or the small tropical tree on which it grows

a In pairs, take turns to read the poem aloud. Choose appropriate expression and tone.

b Who is the voice and character in this poem?

c How would you describe this character? Playful, helpful, destructive, silly or sad?

d What do we call this type of figurative language?

Key word

tone: the quality, pitch and strength of a sound

Language focus

Personification is an indirect way of comparing non-living things with humans, giving human qualities to non-human things. Personification and metaphors are similar because they compare things indirectly. Personification gives figurative rather than literal meaning.

Example: Spring danced in the sun's rays. Summer slept lazily on a bed of blossoms. Autumn fretted about nervously. Winter arrived without warning, demanding my attention.

e   Use these questions to analyse the poem's structure.

- How many stanzas are there?

- Are any words or lines repeated?

- Does the poem have a rhyming pattern?

- Is punctuation used in any specific or unusual ways?

- What effect do the structure and punctuation have on the mood or atmosphere?

f   Update your reading log with the poem 'Wind'. Comment on the difference between poems that rhyme and those that do not. Which do you prefer?

2   Practise personification.

a   Identify words that show a human action or feeling linked to things in nature:

- The sun scowled harshly on the dry land.

- Dark clouds grumbled as they gathered together.

- Autumn leaves surrendered to winter.

- Two trees danced happily in the wind.

- The furious wind rushed around in a rage.

Key word

evoke: make someone remember something or feel an emotion

b   What mood or feeling does each sentence evoke?

c   Add four more lines to the poem 'Wind' to show how else the wind could behave.

Example: I danced with a whirligig and sent it spinning through the air

I played hide-and-seek with a butterfly

d   In groups, put your lines together to create a new poem to perform in the next session.

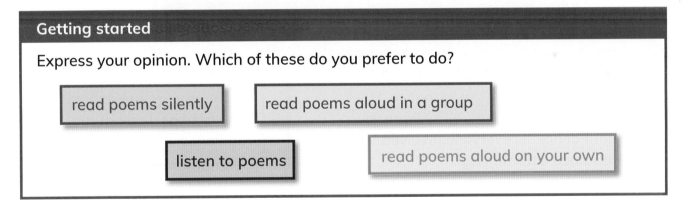

Do you find it helpful to build on the structure of another poem, or do you prefer to write a poem from scratch?

› 3.6 Practise and perform

We are going to ...

- **choose, practise and perform a poem in a group.**

Getting started

Express your opinion. Which of these do you prefer to do?

read poems silently	read poems aloud in a group

listen to poems	read poems aloud on your own

1   Work together to plan and practise a performance.

a   As a class, discuss what makes a good performance.
List five criteria to guide this activity.

b   Get into small groups.

- Choose a poem from Session 3.5 to perform.
Use 'Wind' by Dionne Brand, or the version that you wrote.

- Read it aloud and discuss how you could perform it as a choral verse.

- Decide who will read which part of the poem. Make notes.

c   Practise reading the poem aloud.

2 Perform the poem in front of an audience.

a As a class, decide on an audience and a venue. Would you prefer to perform in front of your class in the classroom, or in front of the whole school?

b Before you perform, check: *How big is the audience? Is there enough space for the audience and the performers? Can everyone see and hear?*

c Perform your poems with confidence, expression and lots of fun.

Let's have the whole group reading the first line.

We can read the next line in pairs.

And the last line on our own.

How are we doing?

Watch and enjoy each performance. Does each group speak clearly, with expression and confidence? Is everyone involved? Is the performance entertaining?

Speaking tip

Remember to use expression and actions. Look at the audience, speak clearly and enjoy yourself.

Look what I can do!

☐ I can identify similes, metaphors and personification in poems.

☐ I can identify key features of a haiku.

☐ I can use different words for effect.

☐ I can plan, write and edit a haiku poem.

☐ I can analyse a poem's language and structure.

☐ I can practise and perform a poem as a choral reading.

Check your progress

1 Explain the meaning of these figurative language terms:

   a simile

   b metaphor

   c personification.

2 Decide what figurative language is used in these sentences, then explain what each one means:

   a No man is an island.

   b Time waits for no one.

   c The time slipped through my fingers like sand through an hourglass.

3 Write three features of a haiku poem.

4 How many syllables are in each of the following words?

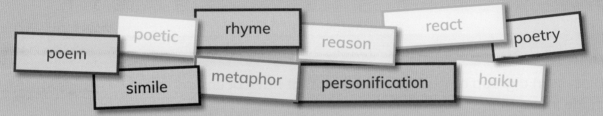

5 Explain these terms and give an example of each:

   a a monosyllabic word

   b a polysyllabic word.

Projects

Group project: choose a cycle, like spring, summer, autumn, winter, or an egg, a caterpillar, a cocoon, a butterfly, and write a haiku to reflect each stage of the cycle. Illustrate and present your poems.

Pair project: draw up a table of figurative language techniques, such as metaphors or alliteration, and give an explanation of each with an example.

Solo project: using poetry anthologies or the internet, choose a haiku and use it to explain the rules for how to write a haiku. Present it as an annotated diagram using the haiku as the example.

4 ▶ Telling timeless tales

> 4.1 Make predictions about a classic tale

We are going to …

- read a book blurb, predict characters' personalities and build a character-profile paragraph.

Getting started

Discuss in a group any books you know that have been made into a film.

1 Which did you read or see first?

2 How were they similar or different?

3 Which version did you prefer?

1   Make predictions based on clues and your own knowledge.

a   Read the following book blurb. Who is the audience for this writing?

The Jungle Book

The Jungle Book by Rudyard Kipling was written in 1892. The book is full of tales of Indian jungle animals, Bagheera the panther, Baloo the bear, Shere Khan the evil tiger and Kaa the **python**, among others, and Mowgli, the man-cub (boy) **fostered** by wolves after Bagheera saved him from Shere Khan as a baby. The stories follow Mowgli's fearless adventures while learning the Law of the Jungle from Baloo and Bagheera. In the end, he learns that he is truly Man and not a wolf. Mowgli gradually becomes a brave hero and leader after he learns the secret of the red flower – fire – something that terrifies the animals, even Shere Khan.

This famous, much loved book has been adapted into both plays and films.

b   Is the text mostly fact or opinion?
Explain your answer using evidence from the text.

c   Predict the genre of *The Jungle Book*, giving reasons and using evidence from the book blurb.

d   Is the *secret of the red flower* literal or figurative language? Give reasons.

e   Based on your knowledge of animal stereotypes, with a partner, discuss and predict the animals' personalities. Use a mind map to organise your ideas. Share and compare your ideas with another pair.

Glossary

python: large snake that kills other animals by coiling itself tightly around them

fostered: looked after a child as part of your family for a time

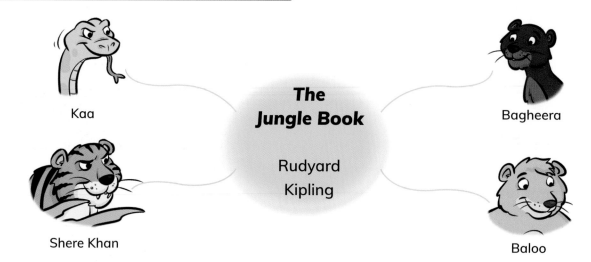

2 Build a character profile of Mowgli.

a Discuss Mowgli's character in a group. Use the adjectives and phrases in the boxes to build a character profile of Mowgli. Add some words and phrases of your own.

b Do you think everyone would share the same opinion of Mowgli?

c Write your character profile of Mowgli in a paragraph, including an opinion on what it would be like to meet him.

Mowgli is a 12-year-old boy who ...

How are we doing?

Swap your paragraph with a partner and check for:

- spelling, grammar and punctuation errors
- sense and flow
- word choice.

> 4.2 Read some classic literature

We are going to ...

- listen to information about classic literature, read and compare two extracts, and explore their features.

Getting started

1   Explain to a partner what you think classic literature means.

2   Make a list of books you think could be regarded as classics.

3   Share your ideas as a class.

20 1   Listen to two authors explaining why it is good for everyone to read classic literature, then answer the following questions.

> **Listening tip**
>
> Read the questions *before* listening so you know what details to listen out for.

a List four characteristics of classic books?

b How can we learn about history from classic books?

c Why do classic books appeal to all sorts of different people?

d What other themes have you come across in books you have read?

e Why do both young and older people enjoy classic literature?

2 Read aloud two extracts from different versions of *The Jungle Book* with a partner.

Mowgli Says Goodbye

The fire was burning furiously at the end of the branch, and Mowgli struck right and left round the circle, and the wolves ran howling with the sparks burning their fur. At last there were only Akela, Bagheera, and perhaps ten wolves that had taken Mowgli's part. Then something began to hurt Mowgli inside him, as he had never been hurt in his life before, and he caught his breath and sobbed, and the tears ran down his face.

"What is it? What is it?" he said. "I do not wish to leave the jungle, and I do not know what this is. Am I dying, Bagheera?"

"No, Little Brother. Those are only tears such as men use," said Bagheera. "Now I know **thou art** a man, and a man's cub no longer. The jungle is shut indeed to **thee henceforward**. Let them fall, Mowgli; they are only tears." So Mowgli sat and cried as though his heart would break; and he had never cried in all his life before.

"Now," he said, "I will go to men. But first I must say farewell to my mother"; and he went to the cave where she lived with Father Wolf, and he cried on her coat, while the four cubs howled miserably.

"**Ye** will not forget me?" said Mowgli.

"Never while we can follow a trail," said the cubs. "Come to the foot of the hill when thou art a man, and we will talk to thee; and we will come into the crop-lands to play with thee by night."

"Come soon!" said Father Wolf. "Oh, wise little Frog, come again soon; for we be old, **thy** mother and I."

"Come soon" said Mother Wolf, "little naked son of mine; for, listen, child of man, I loved thee more than ever I loved my cubs."

"I will surely come," said Mowgli; "and when I come it will be to lay out Shere Khan's **hide** upon the Council Rock. Do not forget me! Tell them in the jungle never to forget me!"

The dawn was beginning to break when Mowgli went down the hillside alone to the crops to meet those mysterious things that are called men.

Rudyard Kipling

Glossary

thou art: old-fashioned way of saying you are

thee: old-fashioned way of saying you (as object)

henceforward: from now on

ye: old fashioned way of saying you (as subject)

thy: old-fashioned way of saying your

hide: animal skin

Mowgli Says Goodbye

Mowgli:	Must I carry fire with me all my life? (*Throws down burning branch.*) Must I always live in fear? (*Panting and sobbing.*) What is it? What's wrong with me? I don't want to leave the jungle and I don't know what this is. Why is my face wet? Am I ill, Baloo? Bagheera, am I dying?
Bagheera (*gently*):	No, Mowgli. Those are only tears such as men use … Let them fall … Let them fall …
Mowgli:	Must I … Must I go?
Akela:	Man goes to Man. It is the way of things.
Mowgli:	Then I go to meet those mysterious things called men … But my mother … Where is my mother?
Enter Raksha.	
Raksha:	My little frog …
Mowgli:	You will not forget me?

99

He embraces Raksha.

Akela: Never while we can follow a trail. You came here for me, my brave son, and so look for me sometimes by night. We may talk by the edge of the fields.

Mowgli: My thanks, great Akela ... Mother Raksha?

Raksha: There is my milk in your blood. Your heart beat next to mine on cold nights in the **lair** ... I lay between you and the teeth of Shere Khan before you could walk ... I love you as my own ... Eat, drink and be strong ... Be strong ...

Mowgli: You have made me strong ... All of you ... Goodbye ... Goodbye ...

He goes. Bagheera, Baloo, Akela and Raksha make their farewell to Mowgli.

Adapted for stage by Stuart Paterson

Glossary

lair: place where a wild animal lives (especially wolves), often underground and hidden

Reading tip

When you read each person's part, try to imagine their expression and gestures, even beyond the stage directions.

Work in a group

a What do you notice about the two extracts?

b Make a list of features of the two extracts. Are there any similarities?

Extract 1 – the book	Extract 2 – the play
Organised into paragraphs	Stage directions in brackets and italics

c   Discuss which version you prefer and share your ideas with another pair.

> 4.3 Develop your language skills

We are going to ...

- practise subject-verb agreement and explore standard English for narrative.

Getting started

1   Work with a partner and remind each other of the different sentence types.

2   What punctuation is used with each sentence type?

3   What other rules are there for forming sentences?

1 Look at how sentences work.

Language focus

Standard English – sentence subjects and verbs

- The subject of a sentence means who or what is *being, having* or *doing* the action.
- The verb must agree with the subject: if the subject is singular, so is the verb; if the subject is plural, so is the verb.

Singular subjects	Plural subjects
I	*we*
you	*you* (can be singular or plural, depending on context)
he/she/it	*they*

Examples: Shere Khan challenges Akela.

(singular subject = Shere Khan = he)

Mowgli and the wolves defend themselves.

(plural subject = Mowgli and the wolves = they)

Either/or and **neither/nor** can be tricky!

Either/or and **neither/nor** are singular if each subject is singular or plural if each subject is plural:

<u>Either</u> Shere Khan <u>or</u> Akela is stronger. <u>Neither</u> the wolves <u>nor</u> the jackals **are** howling.

(= Either <u>Shere Khan is stronger</u> or <u>Akela is stronger</u>.)

(= Neither <u>the wolves are howling</u> nor <u>the jackals are howling</u>.)

If one subject is singular and one is plural, the verb agrees with the closest subject.

<u>Either</u> Mowgli <u>or</u> the wolves **are** going to fight Shere Khan. (plural subject is closest to the verb)

Key word

standard English: written and spoken English that follows the general rules of grammar and punctuation

a Are the subjects in these sentences singular or plural?

- *Mowgli sat and cried as though his heart would break.*
- *Bagheera and Baloo looked after Mowgli.*
- *I lay between you and the teeth of Shere Khan.*
- *Never while we can follow a trail.*
- *Your heart beat next to mine on cold nights.*

b Which form of the verb to be is correct in each sentence?

- *I am / are sure that I will be safe with men!*
- *Akela was / were the leader of the wolf pack.*
- *The wolves was / were sad about Mowgli leaving.*
- *Either Bagheera or Baloo is / are crying.*
- *Neither the wolves nor the hunters was / were as brave as Mowgli.*

2 Look more closely at standard English.

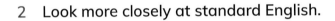

Language focus

Standard English is used in formal narrative writing, although standard English rules can be broken in dialogue. In standard English:

- subjects must agree with verbs
- sentences need correct punctuation according to sentence type: statement, question or command
- capital letters are used at the beginning of a sentence, at the start of dialogue and for proper nouns and adjectives
- apostrophes must be correctly placed to show possession for singular and plural nouns or contractions.

a How many sentence types can you find in the extract from *The Jungle Book*? Give examples of each.

b Invent at least one sentence of each type using the word *Mowgli*.

c Find two examples of an apostrophe to show possession. Are they for singular or plural nouns?

d   Make a list of the proper nouns in the extract.

e   Which verb is correct in these sentences?

- Mowgli *cries / cry* his first tears.

- The cubs *howls / howl* miserably.

f   Write two sentences of your own, one with a singular subject and one with a plural subject. Use correct punctuation.

g   Give examples of when standard English might not be used.

> 4.4 Develop a viewpoint

We are going to ...

- **use detail to understand the text more deeply, explore dialogue and role play a conversation using old-fashioned language.**

Getting started

1   With a partner, list the differences between a play script and a book.

- How are they laid out?

- How do you know what the characters are doing or feeling?

- How can you tell what expression characters are speaking with?

2   Share your ideas as a class and build a list of different conventions for each text type.

1   Writers do not always tell you everything directly; sometimes they show you instead.

Work in groups to discuss these questions. Use evidence from both extracts.

a   Which details show Mowgli has never cried before?

b Mowgli has just scared away Shere Khan with fire and saved his father from being killed, so why do you think he is so upset?

c Why do you think the jungle is now closed to Mowgli?

d What shows how close Mowgli was to his wolf family?

e What tells you Mowgli does not know anything about people?

f Send a spokesperson from your group to summarise your views to another group and report back their ideas.

2 The characters have an unusual style of speaking.

a In groups of five, read the dialogue only in the story extract from *The Jungle Book* in Session 4.2.

b Discuss the answers to these questions, then write the answers in your notebook, checking your spelling, punctuation and grammar carefully.

- How would you describe the way the characters speak? Choose evidence from the text to back up your opinion.

formal   old-fashioned   polite   informal   respectful   impolite

- Is it how you would expect Mowgli and his friends and family to speak to each other?

- What words do they use that you would not use today?

- How does the way the characters speak in the extract compare with the play script dialogue?

- Which extract do you find easier to understand? Give reasons.

- Would readers have found the language unusual if they read it at the time the text was written?

c   With a partner, role play a scene in which Mowgli goes down to the village to join the mysterious 'men'. Speak in the way they do in the story extract in Session 4.2.

- Whom does he meet?
- What does he ask?
- What do they want to know?

d   Write down your role play in the correct format clearly and legibly once you are happy with it.

Speaking tip

Remember how Mowgli speaks and try to use body language that suits how he feels in this new situation.

How easy or hard was it to show Mowgli's feelings in his situation?
How could you improve your role play?

> 4.5 Build a short screenplay

We are going to ...

- compare books, play scripts and film scripts, interpret a cartoon strip and write a short **screenplay**.

Getting started

1   What can a book and film do that a play cannot?

2   What extra things do the actors, director, producers and camera people have to think about in a film rather than a play?

3   Share your ideas as a class.

1   We understand characters in books from the narrative and dialogue. In films, we find out about them from how they act, move and speak.

> **Key word**
>
> **screenplay:** a script for a film including dialogue and descriptions of characters and sets

a   Have you ever seen a film or play based on a story you have read?

- Were the characters the same as you imagined them from the book? Explain.

- Was the plot the same?
  Was anything added in or left out?

- Which version did you prefer? Why?

b   *The Jungle Book* story has been made into films and a play.
Which picture matches your idea of Mowgli and why?

c   Would you prefer to see an animated or a real-life version of this story?

d   How is a film different or similar to a play?

e   How do you think a film script would differ from or be similar to a play script?

Key word

animated: where drawings and models seem to move (in a film)

2   Cartoon strips use speech bubbles and pictures to tell the story.

a   How do you know whether a cartoon character is thinking or speaking?

b   What other visual effects give out information?

c   How does Mowgli feel in the final frame? How would you show if he was happy?

Key word

storyboard: (in films and television) a series of drawings or images showing the planned order of images

3 Film scripts are often planned using storyboards, like cartoons, to work out where actors will stand and move. The final film script includes some of this information as directions for the actors, director and camera people.

   a   Read this film script which is based on the cartoon sequence.

Extract from a film script for *The Jungle Book*

(Mowgli stands alone outside the hut, clutching his fire pot while thinking aloud and scratching his head.)

Mowgli: I wonder what I will find inside. Will they be as kind to me as my wolf family? *(The hut door opens with a thud as Mowgli enters framed in the doorway and drops the fire pot which shatters on the floor. The villagers in the hut look up in surprise.)*

Villager 1:   Who are you?

Villager 2:   Where have you come from?

Villager 3:   Where are your clothes?

(Mowgli moves forward and drops to a crouch, looking confused with his head bowed – camera close-up on Mowgli's face)

---

   b   How is this script similar to the cartoon strip?

   c   Explain to each other how the film script works.

   d   Using film script **conventions**, write the next part of the screenplay.

   e   Test your script by reading it out loud, first in your group and then to another group. Improve the directions and words.

Glossary

conventions: usual and accepted ways of behaving or doing something

---

How are we doing?

Did the group write convincing dialogue? Did you include helpful directions for the actors, director and camera people?

> 4.6 Explore your knowledge of classic tales

We are going to ...

- explore classic tales, skim read an extract and categorise features of timeless tales.

Getting started

Myths and legends are classic tales. They have been told for hundreds of years.

1   What are their features?

2   How are they similar or different?

3   Give examples of each to share with the class.

1   Do you enjoy tales about impossible tasks and fearless heroes?

   a   Discuss the myths and legends you know.

   b   List your favourite legendary heroes and mythical creatures.

   c   • Do you know them from books, films or television?

      • Do you think there is any truth in the stories?

      • How do you think the stories came about?

   d   Summarise for a partner one of your favourite myths or legends.

      • Who are the characters?

      • What is the problem, complication or challenge?

      • How is it resolved?

How are we doing?

How well did you and your partner summarise the story?
Did you identify all the story stages?

2 In fiction, the author can make any character the storyteller.

a In small groups, skim read the following extract from a modern retelling of Ancient Greek myths.

- What does the narrator say he is and he is not?

- What evidence in the story supports what he says?

- Would you believe someone who told you this? Why?

b Who is being welcomed in this extract?

Did you know that Mount Olympus is the highest mountain in Greece with its summit often covered in clouds? Why do you think the ancient Greek gods made Olympus their home?

Reading tip

When you skim read, focus on key words and phrases to help you identify the main idea.

Welcome to Olympus

Well, you have opened my book. You have turned the page. You are now in Ancient Greece, and you are standing on my mountain.

You had better come up.

No, I am not a ghost.

NO, I am not a giant.

I am a god. Yes, a god!

But come up higher, so we don't have to shout. I am tired of shouting.

Steep, isn't it? Too steep for most people. And the air is so thin, you may get out of breath. Take your time. I'm in no hurry.

There! You made it! Welcome! Welcome to Mount Olympus. Have you ever climbed so high? Or looked out across such vast distances? Or stood so far above the Earth?

Sit down! Choose a rock and make yourself comfortable.

And now I will tell you who I am ...

I am Zeus, the great god, Zeus.

Zeus the all-bright, they call me.

Zeus, the bringer of light.

Yes, I am Zeus, and I rule over all other gods and goddesses.

There now, up in the sky are two of my children: **Apollo** wheeling the sun away till tomorrow morning, and **Artemis** rolling out the moon.

And the winged horse over there?

That's Pegasus.

He takes me in my **chariot** wherever I want to go. I'll tell you more about him and Apollo and Artemis later.

Jenny Koralek

Glossary

Apollo: Greek god of the sun, poetry and music and healing; son of Zeus and Leto; twin brother of Artemis

Artemis: Greek goddess of the hunt and the moon; daughter of Zeus and Leto; twin sister of Apollo (known as Diana in Roman mythology)

chariot: vehicle with two wheels that was used in races and fights in ancient times and was pulled by a horse

3 Myths and legends come from the oral storytelling tradition.

a Which card do you think describes a myth and which a legend?

A	B
Stories passed from person to person based on something that once possibly happened, with heroic characters, fantastical places and unlikely events. The plot focuses on a main character who overcomes difficulties – often a monster. They can also be about places, objects and animals.	Stories set in the ancient past to explain the world and events that people did not understand, such as floods, earthquakes or how the world began. The plot often involves gods or supernatural beings and unbelievable events not based on anything factual.

b Which of the following titles sound like myths and which legends?

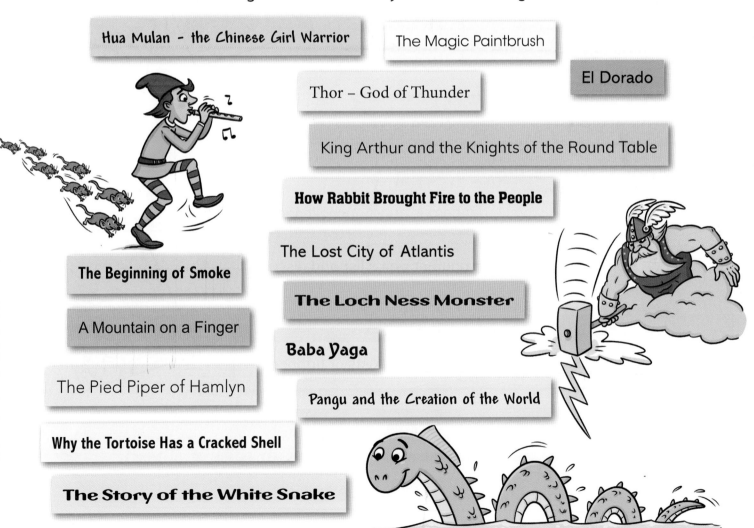

Hua Mulan - the Chinese Girl Warrior

The Magic Paintbrush

El Dorado

Thor – God of Thunder

King Arthur and the Knights of the Round Table

How Rabbit Brought Fire to the People

The Lost City of Atlantis

The Beginning of Smoke

The Loch Ness Monster

A Mountain on a Finger

Baba Yaga

The Pied Piper of Hamlyn

Pangu and the Creation of the World

Why the Tortoise Has a Cracked Shell

The Story of the White Snake

c   Sort these features into two lists in your notebook: **Myths** and **Legends**.
Remember, some features may appear in both lists.

Any volunteers? Can you
retell a myth or legend from
your culture or region?

Gods and goddesses

Heroes and villains

Timeless   **May be based on a historical event**

Explains a natural **phenomenon**

Set long ago   **Fantastical creatures**

Superhuman or unlikely powers

Unlikely or exaggerated events

A classic opening, e.g. *Long, long ago ...*

A dangerous quest or challenge

d   Compare your list with another pair's list and discuss
any differences.

Glossary

phenomenon: something unusual that exists or happens

What was difficult about identifying myths and legends?
What features can you use to help you decide?

› 4.7 Explore the text

We are going to ...

- explore narrative voice and discuss features of dialogue.

Getting started

Explain to a partner the difference between first- and third-person narrative.

1   What are the features of each, including the pronouns and possessive adjectives used?

2   What are the advantages and disadvantages of each?

3   Share your ideas as a class.

1   Choosing who will tell the story is an important decision for a writer.

a   Think about the narrator of the extract *Welcome to Olympus* in session 4.6.

- How can you tell who the narrator is?

- Is the extract in first-person or third-person narrative?

- Find examples that show the narrator's personal views and feelings.

b   The narrator of this book tells a series of tales chapter by chapter. Thinking about who the narrator is, write a short paragraph to explain the type of stories you think the narrator will tell. Give your reasons.

c   What might an outside or third-person narrator be able to say that a character could not say?

Reading tip

Look at the pronouns in the narrative to help you decide on narrative voice. *We, I, my* and *our* indicate first-person narrative; *they, he/she/it, their, his/her* and *its* indicate third-person narrative.

d   Scan the extract to find two or three parts that would change if it was narrated by an outside or third-person narrator.

- Read the extract aloud, changing details to make it sound as if an outside or third-person narrator tells the story.

- Make a list of things that had to change.

e   Do you prefer books written in the first or the third person? Jot down some notes and discuss your views with a partner. Ask each other questions to find out why.

2   Dialogue is often informal in style because it shows how the characters speak.

Work in a group.

a   What is your impression of Zeus from the extract?

- List some adjectives to describe him.

- Will he make a good storyteller for the book? Why?

b   Why do Mount Olympus, Apollo, Artemis, Pegasus and Zeus have capital letters?

c   The extract reads like dialogue, but it is punctuated like narrative.

- What features make it seem like dialogue rather than narrative?

- Is this an enticing way to begin a book?

d   Exchange your views with another group by swapping a volunteer. Do you agree?

e   Add the extract to your reading log. Explain whether you think you would enjoy reading more of this book.

> 4.8 Direct and reported speech

We are going to ...

- explore direct and indirect speech, and understand the punctuation and grammar of indirect speech.

Getting started

Work with a partner.

1 One of you tell the other something starting with: I am going to ...

2 The other tells the first speaker what they said they were going to do, starting with: You were going to ...

3 Discuss how the pronouns and tenses change, and share ideas as a class on how direct speech changes when someone reports it.

1 Discuss the differences between direct and reported speech.

Language focus

Direct speech records the actual words the characters say.

When someone reports what someone else said, we call it **reported** or **indirect speech**.

Direct speech	Indirect speech
Zeus announced, 'This is my mountain.'	Zeus announced **that** it was his mountain.
'You are in **Ancient Greece**,' said Zeus.	Zeus said **that** we were in Ancient Greece.

a Use the examples above to find differences.
Use these words: speech marks, verb tense and that.

b   Take turns in groups of three.

   • Privately, tell one person what you did at the weekend.

   • That person tells the third person what you did.

      • Did everyone report what was said accurately?

      • Did the pronouns change? (*I* to *he* or *she*)

      • Did you use the past tense? *He or she said that ...*

      • How does the communication change when it is reported?

c   Write these sentences in your notebook in direct speech.

   Example: Zeus said that he was in no hurry.

            'I am in no hurry,' said Zeus.

   • Zeus said that he had many children.

   • Zeus explained that Pegasus was his winged horse.

   • Zeus complained that he was tired of shouting.

2   Change direct speech into indirect speech.

a   Write these sentences as indirect speech using correct punctuation.

   Example: 'I am the ruler of the gods,' said Zeus.
            Zeus said that he was the ruler of the gods.

> **Writing tip**
>
> Watch out for pronouns. They're different in reported speech!

   • Zeus said, 'I am a god.'

   • 'No,' confirmed Zeus, 'I am not a ghost.'

   • 'Pegasus pulls my chariot,' Zeus explained.

b   With a partner, invent a dialogue between Zeus and one of his listeners. Write it out in indirect speech.

〉 4.9 Check your knowledge

We are going to ...

- **predict a classic story genre, identify a myth or legend and work with nouns.**

Getting started

Why the Hippo Has No Hair is a story from Kenya. Before reading the story, imagine how hippos lost their hair. In a group:

1　predict the main idea of the story

2　explain whether it sounds like a myth or a legend.

1　Myths and legends can be classified by their key features.

   a　Read *Why the Hippo Has No Hair* as a group to check your predictions.

      - Make notes on features of myths or legends you notice.

      - Decide if the story is a myth or a legend, using examples from the story.

   b　What is the feeling or mood in this story? How has the writer created it?

   c　Are the events in this story likely? Why?

   d　How is this story similar to or different from a fable?

   e　Do good stories have to be true to life?
Give examples from a range of stories that you know.

Why the Hippo Has No Hair – a story from Kenya

Once upon a time, Hippo and Fire were friends. They used to meet each other in the forest and talk all night. It wasn't dark because the fire's light was very bright.

One day, Hippo asked Fire to visit him.

"Thank you very much," said Fire. "Can I come tomorrow?"

"That will be very nice," said Hippo.

The two friends said goodbye to each other, then they went home.

The next day came. Fire did not wake up until the middle of the morning. Then he got up and began to walk to Hippo's house.

Suddenly, he saw a bush running away from him.

"Why are you running away?" asked Fire.

"You know why I am running away," answered Bush. "Look! The grass is running away too."

The fire was very near and Bush was beginning to get very hot.

"I must go," said Bush. "You are hurting me. You are too hot! And you are hurting the little animals who live in me."

"Wait for me !" called Fire. "I'll come with you."

Bush saw Fire running towards him. He tried to run but it was too late. Fire ate him and all the little animals too.

Fire went on walking towards Hippo's house. When he went near bushes or grass, they ran away. If they did not run away very fast, Fire ate them.

Hippo was in his house, waiting for his friend. He looked out of the door and saw Fire eating the bushes and the grass. Hippo was afraid. When Fire saw Hippo, he called, "I'm coming!"

Hippo went to meet his friend. "Come into my house," he said.

Fire went in and looked round the inside of the house.

"This is a very comfy house," said Fire. "I like it."

When they were both in the house, Fire was very near Hippo, who was too hot, but he didn't want to be unkind to his friend.

"Where shall I sit?" asked Fire.

"On my bed," answered Hippo.

But Hippo's bed was made of dry grass. When Fire sat on it, he burnt it.

Fire caught Hippo's hair, which started to burn.

Hippo tried to run to the river but he was running very slowly. All the time, his hair was burning.

"Help! Help!" he shouted.

In the end, he got to the river and jumped into the water. At last, he was safe. The fire wasn't burning him. He wasn't too hot and he was very comfortable in the river.

But all Hippo's hair was gone. And it didn't grow again. It never grew again at all.

Why do hippos never go far from water? Why do they have no hair?

Now you know the answers to these questions.

Retold by Pamela Kola

How are we doing?

Did you recognise the key features of myths and legends? Could you tell if the story is a myth or a legend?

2   **Classify** nouns.

Language focus

Nouns are naming words for people, places and things.
There are four types of nouns:

- **Common nouns:** These name animals, objects and things,
  e.g., *fire and hippopotamus.*

- **Proper nouns:** These name specific people and places and start
  with a capital letter, e.g., *Pamela Kola*

- **Abstract nouns:** These name things we cannot see, touch, hear,
  taste, or smell. They are something we experience like an idea or
  an emotion, e.g., *happiness, freedom, generosity.*

- **Collective nouns:** These name groups of things or common nouns,
  e.g., *a swarm of bees, a pack of cards, a flock of birds.*

a   Scan *Why the Hippo Has No Hair* for different types of nouns.
    Write down examples of the types you find.

b   Explain why Hippo, Fire and Bush have capital letters.

c   Write down a collective noun for each of the nouns Hippo, Fire and Bush.

Writing tip

Some nouns have well-known collective nouns that go with them.
If you don't know the collective noun, invent one to suit the animals
or things you are describing.

d   Abstract nouns are often similar to their related adjectives.

Examples: *angry – anger; jealousy – jealous, thoughtfulness – thoughtful;
sympathy – sympathetic*

- Write the abstract nouns that are related to these adjectives:

hateful   peaceful   beautiful   honest
disappointed   patient   democratic

e   Explain how the adjectives are formed from the nouns.

- Can you think of other adjectives formed in a similar way?

- Write the adjectives that are related to these abstract nouns:

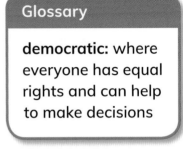

Glossary

democratic: where everyone has equal rights and can help to make decisions

sensitivity   fear   sorrow   trust
anxiety   friendship   chaos

f   Write three abstract nouns that reflect Hippo's and Fire's feelings during the story.

g   Add *Why the Hippo Has No Hair* to your reading log and comment on whether you enjoyed it and why.

> 4.10 Work with words

We are going to ...

- explore plural spellings, identify countable and uncountable nouns, and explore quantifiers.

Getting started

Discuss with a partner.

1 Can all nouns be singular and plural? Give examples to each other.

2 Explain how you create plural nouns. Do all nouns follow the same rules? Give examples.

3 Share your answers as a class.

1 Most nouns are *countable*, which means they can be singular or plural. The plural form of most nouns is formed by adding *s*: cat – cats. Other nouns form the plural in different ways.

I can count countable nouns – one egg, two eggs, three eggs ... I can't do that with water!

a   If the word ends in **ch**, **sh**, **ss** or **x**, add **es** to form the plural. Write some sentences using these nouns in their plural form: *fox, glass, box, wish, match.*

b   If the words end in **o**, add **s** or **es** to form the plural.

- If the final **o** comes after a consonant, add **es**. Write these words and their plural forms in your notebook:

- If the final **o** comes after a vowel, add **s**. Write these words and their plural forms in your notebook:

c   When nouns end in **f** or **fe**, change the **f** or **fe** to **v** and add **es** to form the plural: *hoof → hooves.*

- Write these words and their plural forms in your notebook.

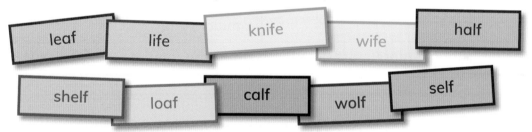

- There are exceptions to this rule: *chief – chiefs, belief – beliefs, roof – roofs, reef – reefs, safe – safes.* Add these words to your spelling log.

- Choose two f or fe words – one regular and one exception – and use them in sentences of your own.

2   Quantifiers with countable and uncountable nouns.

a   Write these sentences in your notebook choosing the correct quantifier.

- Have you got *any / several* rice?

- You must wait a *few / little* minutes.

- The choir sang *much / many* songs today.

- Anwar used a large *number / amount* of sugar in his cooking.

- You ought to put *fewer / less* milk in your tea.

b Write sentences of your own using the quantifiers in the boxes.

most | a few | many | much | enough

Language focus

Quantifiers are words or groups of words that appear before a noun indicating a non-specific quantity. They can be used with countable and uncountable (mass) nouns.

With uncountable nouns	With countable nouns
e.g. *flour, pepper, earth, mud, tea, rice*	e.g. *eggs, chairs, snakes, houses, shoes*
much	many
a little / little / very little	a few / few / very few / fewer
a bit of	a number of
a great deal of	several
a large amount of	a large number of
a large quantity of	a great number of
less	a majority of

Both: all, enough, more/most, less/least, no, some, any, a lot of, lots of, plenty of

Writing tip

People often confuse *fewer* and *less*. Fewer can only be used with countable nouns like *tomatoes* or *potatoes*. You **can't** say *fewer water* or *fewer salt*. You need to use *less – less sand, less sugar*, etc.

3 This storyteller uses various techniques to bring the story to life.

a Find any exclamations in the text.

• How you can tell they are exclamations?

• What atmosphere or mood do the exclamations create?

b Why do you think bushes and grass are given human characteristics? How does this add to the effect?

c Re-read the story in your group, making it as much fun as you can.

- Emphasise the exclamations to add urgency.
- Bring the characters to life by adding accents or unusual ways of speaking.
- Use expression and body language.

Speaking tip

Remember that these stories were told long before they were ever written down. The way the story is told is as important as the story itself.

How are we doing?

Did groups find an interesting way to interpret the story? Did they use expression and body language to make it fun for the audience?

> 4.11 and 4.12 Write your own classic tale to tell

We are going to ...

- **revise classic tale features, rewrite a classic tale and present it to an audience.**

Getting started

1 Do you know any classic tales from your region?

2 Retell one to a partner.

3 Be prepared to share your retelling with the class.

1 Anyone who retells a classic tale can bring something new to the story.

a Compare the classic tales you know with the fact files below. Do they match?

Long, long ago …

Myths fact file
• Classic opening
• Set in the ancient past or timeless
• Explains a natural phenomenon
• No basis in fact
• Gods and fantastical beings
• Characters portraying nature (e.g. wind, rain)
• Unlikely events

Legends fact file
• Classic opening
• Set long ago
• Loosely based on historical events
• A main hero or heroine
• Gods, monsters or powerful enemies
• A seemingly impossible **quest**
• Unlikely events

b Some people think that *The Jungle Book* story is a legend based on historical events.

- What historical event do you think it could be based on?

- Based on the story extract from *The Jungle Book*, what seemingly impossible quest has Mowgli set himself?

> **Key word**
>
> quest: an attempt to get something or do something difficult

2 Retell a story you have read in this unit, or a different one you already know, or invent your own.

a Use a diagram to plan your outline.

Classic tales		
Myths	**Legends**	**Narrative person**
• What is the natural event? • Who are the characters?	• Who is the hero? • What is the task or challenge?	• First person – a character • Third person – an outsider looking in

Myths	Legends	Narrative person
• What are the unlikely events? • How will the plot explain the event?	• What are the unlikely events? • How does she, he or it succeed?	

b   Decide which details or conventions to change.

c   Write your first draft.

- Decide on a *first-person* or *third-person* narrator.

- Use a mixture of *direct* and *reported* speech and make the dialogue interesting and suitable for the characters.

- Add sound effects, exclamations and repetition.

- Use a variety of sentence types.

- Organise your writing into paragraphs for both narrative and dialogue.

d   Read your draft to a partner and listen to their feedback.

- Is the story clearly a myth or a legend?

- Are the key features clear?

- Is it lively and interesting?

e   Make corrections and improvements. Check for:

- standard English in narrative sections

- subject–verb agreement and punctuation of direct speech.

Use the *editing* checklist in the Toolkit **at the back of this book** to help you improve, as well as dictionaries and thesauruses.

You could make the hero into a heroine or have a different challenge.

3 Storytelling is a skill that improves with practice.

    a Practise telling your story using expression to add drama.

    b Hold a storytelling event and enjoy telling and hearing each other's stories.

    c Give each other feedback on the story and the telling of it.

Speaking tip

Make notes in your story to remind you where and how to add emphasis and special effects.

What did you find easy and hard about retelling a story?

How could you improve your writing and your storytelling?

Look what I can do!

☐ I can build a character profile in a paragraph.

☐ I can list and compare the features of different text types.

☐ I can write and improve a short screenplay.

☐ I can differentiate between and write direct and reported speech.

☐ I can present a dramatic reading of a story.

☐ I can retell a myth, legend or classic tale, changing some of the story elements.

Check your progress

1 Choose a classic tale and write two features of that story type.

2 **a** Rewrite this sentences in reported speech:

Zeus announced, "I am the father of Artemis and Apollo."

b Rewrite this sentence in direct speech:

Zeus proudly told the crowd that his daughter was goddess of the moon.

3 Sort these nouns into the correct columns.

love   chariot   Pegasus   Olympus   respect   mountain

Greece   moon   power

Common nouns	Proper nouns	Abstract nouns

4 Organise these nouns into two lists: countable nouns and uncountable nouns.

pepper   dancing   horse   jungle   happiness

work   football   pen

5 Write down the plural spelling of these words:

bunch   box   flash   wolf

wife   tomato

batch   kangaroo

Projects

Group project: to produce an audio or video version of your retellings from the final session in this unit. Decide whether to have a single narrator or groups taking part. Use props, music and sound effects to bring your tales to life. Record all your stories for another class to listen to or watch.

Pair project: draw up a table to compare different types of timeless tales, such as myths, legends, traditional tales, folklore or any others you choose. Compare features, themes and characters.

Solo project: design a poster to advertise the story you retold in the final session of this unit. Include the title, something to grab attention to persuade people to come and listen to your story and illustrations, hinting at events in the story.

5 ▸ Tell me how

> 5.1 Gather facts

We are going to ...

- listen to an interview and make notes, using key words, and understand figurative expressions.

Getting started

1 What do you know about salt? Can you name any uses for it? Share them with your group.

2 Copy this table into your notebook. Make notes using key words.

3 Fill in the third column as you discover new information.

What I already know	What I would like to know	What I have found out

1 Listen to an audio interview about salt.

> Not all salt is edible. There are many types of salt. It is found all over the Earth and has even been found on Mars!

a   With a partner, recall facts from the audio. Add to your table of information.

b   Is this audio an example of fiction or non-fiction? Explain.

c   In which sections of the library would you find out the following?

where salt is found

how salt is used

what salt is made of

the role of salt in the past

d   What key words would you use to search for this information online?

e   Make a list of questions you would like to ask about salt.

2   Explore expressions

a   In small groups, read the figurative expressions. What images come to mind?

b   Link each expression to its meaning.

c   Use each expression in a sentence to show its meaning.

d   Are any of these expressions based on facts? Give an example.

Even though it's easier and cheaper to buy salt these days, we still use many expressions that come from its value in the past.

e   Share other expressions that you hear or use.
What do they mean?

take it with a pinch of salt

worth one's salt

rub salt into a wound

the salt of the Earth

go back to the **salt mines**

hard-working and valuable

don't take it too seriously

return to work

a very **dependable** person

make someone feel worse

Glossary

salt mine: a mine where rock salt is taken from the ground

dependable: reliable or trustworthy

> 5.2 Read instructions

We are going to ...

- compare language style and purpose, explore an instruction text, and scan for details and specialised vocabulary.

Getting started

1   Work in pairs. Give your partner instructions on how to do one of the following:

play a particular game   solve a maths sum   go somewhere

2   Use clear, precise language. Order your instructions.

1   Discuss the style and purpose of different text types.

Language focus

Style is the way a text is written. The style must fit the purpose of the text.

- **A personal style**
  informal, chatty, relaxed
  colloquial words
  contractions (*I've, it's*)
  first-person pronouns (*I, me, mine*)

- **An impersonal style**
  formal, concise, clear
  specialised vocabulary
  avoids slang or contractions
  uses second- and third-person pronouns (*you, it, they*)

a What is the purpose and style of each of the following text types?

b Comment on how writers choose different writing styles for different texts, e.g., the reason for using an impersonal style.

c Give an example sentence for each text type using first-, second- and third-person narrative.
Match each sentence to the text types.

d Name books or texts that use a mixture of styles.

2 Explore an instruction text.

a Skim read *Make a crystal star*. Name three text features you notice.

Glossary

non-edible: not to be eaten

solution: a liquid with something dissolved in it

evaporate: to turn from liquid to vapour or gas

Make a Crystal Star

Materials

borax powder*	hot water	large glass jar
ice-cream stick	pipe cleaners	food colouring

* Borax (or sodium borate – a type of salt) is a **non-edible** natural mineral used in various products to clean or preserve. You can find it in the laundry section in the supermarket. It can be substituted with alum, bicarbonate of soda or sugar.

Safety tips:

Ask an adult to help you when pouring hot water.

Wash your hands after touching borax.

Steps

1 Use three pipe cleaners.
2 Twist them together to form a six-point star shape.
3 Tie a length of string to one 'point' of the star.
4 Fasten the other end around the middle of an ice-cream stick.
5 Dissolve the borax powder in hot water. Use about three heaped tablespoons of borax per standard cup (250 ml) of water. Keep adding until no more will dissolve.
6 Half fill the jar with the borax **solution**.
7 Add a few drops of food colouring.
8 Place the stick across the top of the jar so the star dangles in the solution.
9 Place the jar in a warm, dry, safe place and don't disturb it.
10 Watch the crystals grow over the next few days.
11 Remove the star when all the solution has **evaporated**. Hang up the star using the string.
12 Use different food colourings to make different coloured stars and hang them inside your window.

What happens

Borax dissolves in hot water.

When the water evaporates, the borax stays behind.

Crystals form as the borax attaches to the pipe cleaner.

b Scan for details. Discuss these questions.

- Is the style personal or impersonal?

- Why did the writer choose this style?

- How many steps are there?
  Is the sequence important?

- Identify the specialised words that you need to understand. Discuss their meanings. Add them to your spelling log and highlight the tricky parts.

c In pairs, repeat the instructions to each other without reading them. Listen to your partner repeat the instructions. Do they make sense?

Reading tip

Before you start following written instructions, read them through and relate them to the diagram to make sure you understand what you will need and what you are going to do.

How are we doing?

Were the steps in the correct order? Were the instructions clear?

d Add these instructions to your reading log and say if you would like to try it out at home. Do all instructions look the same or can you set them out another way?

Name:	Date:

Title: _____

Materials Needed:

_____

_____

_____

Instructions:

1. _____

_____

2. _____

_____

3. _____

_____

4. _____

_____

Title: _____

What you need:

What to do

1.

2.

3.

4.

5.

Date: _____

Title: _____

Step 1

_____

_____

_____

Step 2

_____

_____

_____

Step 3

_____

_____

_____

Step 4

_____

_____

_____

> 5.3 Be clear and direct

We are going to ...

- recall instructional language, use command verbs and replace nouns with pronouns.

Getting started

1   Read the *Make a Crystal Star* instructions in Session 5.2 again.

2   Identify the verbs in each step. What do you notice?

1   Use command verbs.

Language focus

A **simple sentence** has one finite **verb**, a **subject** (the person or thing doing the action), and usually an **object** (what has the action done to it).

Example: <u>The children</u> <u>make</u> <u>salt crystals</u>.

          subject   verb   object

Instructions look as if there is no subject because the subject word is not always included, only implied:

(you) <u>Close</u> the door.

implied subject   verb

A **compound sentence** (which could be a command or instruction) is formed when two simple sentences are joined.

Wash your hands. Wash your face. = Wash your hands and your face.

a   Change these sentences into instructions by starting with a command verb.

Example: Tali will answer the question. <u>Answer</u> the question.

The children do the task individually.

They work in groups today.

They listen carefully to the instructions.

Can you open the door and windows?

You must follow my example and do what I say.

b   Write five of your own commands beginning with a command verb. Make sure at least one is a compound sentence.

2   Use pronouns to avoid repetition.

a   What is the pronoun referring to in these sentences from the instructions in session 5.2?

*   *If hot water is added to borax, <u>it</u> dissolves.*

*   *When <u>it</u> evaporates, the borax stays behind.*

*   *<u>It</u> attaches to the pipe cleaner so crystals form and <u>they</u> grow bigger.*

b   Replace the repeated noun (the subject or object) in each sentence with a pronoun.

Example: Add salt to flavour food or preserve <u>food</u>.
        Add salt to flavour food or preserve <u>it</u>.

> **Writing tip**
>
> When you use a pronoun, check it is clear to what or to whom the pronoun is referring.
>
> *If you add salt to the popcorn, I will eat it. (Is it the salt, the popcorn or both?)*

- Dissolve the borax in hot water and leave the hot, borax water to cool.

- Pour the solution into a jar then place the jar somewhere safe.

- Add the salt and sugar then wait for the salt and sugar to dissolve.

- Add water to each glass then move each glass to a safe spot.

- Once the crystals start to form, leave the crystals to grow.

c Write three command sentences for an instruction text using the third-person pronouns it, they and them.

〉 5.4 Nouns count

We are going to ...

- **recall prepositions, use collective nouns and write command sentences.**

Getting started

1 A preposition can change the meaning of a sentence. A good way to remember prepositions is to think of all the places you can go – into, on, up, under, over, across, against, next to and along.

2 Use these words to make up sentences describing your journey to school.

1   Use prepositions to show position.

   Example: Place the bowl <u>on</u> the <u>table</u>. Place the bowl
       <u>on</u> <u>it</u>. Place the bowl <u>on</u> <u>a flat, even surface</u>.

   a   In pairs, discuss which preposition is demonstrated in
       each picture. Make up a sentence for each picture.

Pour water — behind / under / over / in — the bowl.

> **Writing tip**
>
> A preposition precedes a noun, proper noun, pronoun or noun phrase that it modifies.

> Prepositions are small but very powerful because they can change the meaning of a sentence.

   b   List the prepositions in the salt crystals
       instructions in session 5.2.

   c   Rewrite each sentence using a sensible
       preposition and draw a picture to match it.

   •   Place a sponge (on / in / beside / under) the dish.

   •   Pour hot water (into / over / on / around) the jug.

   •   Place the dish (in / above / on / under) a window ledge.

   •   Throw the leftover solution (into / down / onto / below)
       the drain.

   d   Discuss how to use these tricky prepositions and
       use them in sentences of your own:

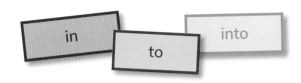

in   to   into

2 Use collective nouns as countable nouns

a   Identify the collective noun in the following items:

the box of cereal   a glass of milk   this pot of soup   a cloud of smoke

b   Use the collective nouns you identified to describe something else.

c   Think of a collective noun to describe the following *uncountable* nouns.

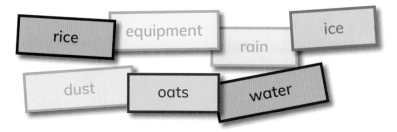

rice   equipment   ice   rain   dust   oats   water

d   Write three command sentences of your own that include:

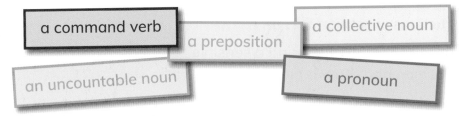

a command verb   a preposition   a collective noun   an uncountable noun   a pronoun

Example: <u>Put</u> <u>a spoon</u> of <u>dishwashing soap</u> <u>into</u> the water and stir <u>it</u>.

> 5.5 and 5.6 Write instructions and demonstrate

We are going to ...

- sequence information, write an instruction and demonstrate a set of instructions.

Getting s tarted

1   In pairs, take turns to give each other instructions on how to do something like plant a tree or cook a meal.

2   Afterwards, discuss what was similar and what was different about your instructions.

1   Write instructions.

a   Work with a partner. Discuss what is happening in the diagram.

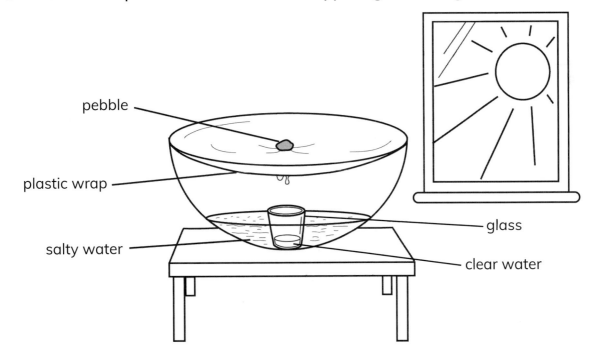

b   Work out and order the steps of the experiment.

c   Together, write instructions to go with the diagram.
Use the features listed in the box to help you.

Features of instructions

- neat layout with headings
- title
- 'how to …'
- list of equipment
- numbered steps
- command verbs
- simple present tense
- correct prepositions
- impersonal style
- second- and third-person pronouns
- collective nouns where useful

d   Share your instructions with another pair.
Discuss ways to improve your instructions.

e   Now make up and write your own instructions for using salt.
Pick your own activity to explain or choose one of the following ideas. Use the pictures to guide you and do some research if you need more details.

- How to use salt and water colours to paint a picture

- How to use salt to brush your teeth

- How to use salt to get a stain out of clothes

f   Use the features listed in the box to guide you as you write instructions.

g   Check and edit your work.
    Ask a partner to check it and offer ideas on ways to improve.

h   Use your own instructions template, or one from your teacher,
    to lay out and write your instructions neatly. It can be handwritten
    or you can use on-screen tools to present it.

> You can work out your own instructions
> or you can do some research first.

2   Demonstrate in front of an audience.

a   Use your written instructions to give a
    demonstration of your chosen experiment
    to the class.

b   The speaking tips will guide you as
    you plan and present.

c   Listen as your peers present.
    Reflect on how well they follow the tips.

Speaking tips

Make sure you have all
the equipment you need.

Prepare and practise the
correct sequence.

Face your audience and
make eye contact.

Speak clearly.

Have a good introduction
and conclusion.

Listening tip

Listen for the order,
the flow and relevant
information. Does it
make sense?

How are we doing?

Watch each other demonstrate and decide if the speaker:

- was confident and clear

- gave step-by-step instructions in the correct order

- included a good introduction and conclusion.

> 5.7 Find out more

We are going to ...

- skim read a text to get an overview, scan a text for details and ask and answer questions.

Getting started

1   In pairs, find synonyms for these words in a thesaurus.

2   Now use them to make sentences.

extreme   diameter   saturated   insulated   immense

1   Skim read the text to get an overview.

   a   Together, view the headings, topic sentences and pictures/diagrams. Note any questions that come to mind as you skim read. Share them with the class.

   b   How would you classify this text – fiction or non-fiction? What is the difference?

   c   List unfamiliar words. If you can't find their definitions in the glossary, use a dictionary.

Key word

topic sentence: a sentence that sums up what the paragraph is about; usually the first sentence, but not always

d Is this an information text, an explanation or both?
Use the table below to explain your answer.

Information text	Explanation text
Describes the *what?*	Explains the *how?* or *why?*
General information	Specific information
Sequence is not essential.	Sequence is important.

e Practise reading the text aloud. Take turns to read it out with accuracy and confidence.

Speaking tip

Use expression in your voice so that your partner can tell which details you find the most interesting.

The Giant Crystal Cave

What is the Giant Crystal Cave?

The Giant Crystal Cave is an underground cave with the largest **selenite** crystals ever found. Until recently, nobody knew it existed. The cave is the size of a football field and as high as a two-storey building. Some of the crystals are over 11 m long, 4 m in diameter and weigh about 50 000 kg. Since the extreme heat and humidity are **lethal**, it is closed to the public. Equally dangerous are the sharp, slippery crystals.

The discovery

The cave was discovered in the year 2000 by miners. They were pumping water out of a mine when they stumbled upon this natural cave 300 m underground. Because the crystals **deteriorate** in air, scientists are working on ways to preserve them.

The location

The Giant Crystal Cave is one of a cluster of natural cavities in the limestone rock near the Naica silver mine in the Chihuahua Desert, Mexico. Other caves in the cluster include:

- **The chamber:** located below the Giant Crystal Cave. It contains hot magma which heats the water in the Giant Crystal Cave.
- **The Cave of Swords:** discovered in 1910, located 120 m above the Giant Crystal Cave. The cave is 70 m in diameter and has crystals up to 2 m in length.
- **The Queen's Eye Cave:** discovered in 2000 at a depth of 300 m. The narrow opening of the cave resembles an eye, hence its name.
- **The Candles Cave:** discovered in 2000 at a depth of 300 m. The crystals have long, delicate structures resembling candles.
- **The Ice Palace:** 150 m below the surface. It was not flooded with water, so it has smaller crystals.

Conditions inside the cave

It is deadly hot in the cave, around 58° C (136° F) – hot enough to cook an egg. A person can survive for only 10 minutes unless they wear protective clothing. When you wear an insulated suit and cold breathing system, you have 45 minutes to explore. Furthermore, the crystals are extremely dangerous because they are sharp and slippery.

How did the crystals form?

According to scientists, there is a simple explanation for how these crystals formed.

Firstly, the ground water heated up in a chamber below the cave. The hot water became saturated with minerals, mainly gypsum.

Over time, this mineral-rich hot water filled the cave.

For thousands of years, the conditions in the cave remained constant.

As a result, the crystals grew to immense sizes.

While submerged, the crystals continued to grow.

Glossary

selenite: the crystallised form of the mineral *gypsum*, also known as *moonstone* because of its colour, brilliance and transparency

lethal: harmful, destructive; causing death

deteriorate: get into a worse condition

2   Read the text for meaning. Answer the questions in your notebook.

   a   When and how was The Giant Crystal Cave discovered?

   b   What is unique about this cave?

   c   Why is it closed to the public?

   d   Would you like to visit The Giant Crystal Cave? Give three reasons.

   e   What do the names tell you about each cave?

   f   Make up some other names to describe each of the caves, based on the information.

   g   In your reading log, note whether you enjoyed reading this non-fiction text and whether you would like to find out more about this cave or other caves.

> 5.8 Make notes

We are going to ...

• **summarise the main idea, make notes and retell information from our notes.**

Getting started

1   Compare The Giant Crystal Cave text in Session 5.7 with the Make a Crystal Star instructions in Session 5.2.

2   What similarities and differences are there?

1   Use a list or a table to summarise.

   a   Together, identify the **topic sentence** in each section of The Giant Crystal Cave text and make a list.

   b   In pairs, copy this table and compare the caves. Use key words only.

Name	Discovered	Location	Description	What's inside?

   c   Now, use your notes from your list or table to give a summary talk to another group about The Giant Crystal Cave. Take turns so everyone has a chance to speak.

2 Use **graphic organisers** to make notes.

a You can use different types of graphic organisers to make notes. Which ones have you used or seen before? Discuss the purpose of each one – what they can be used for.

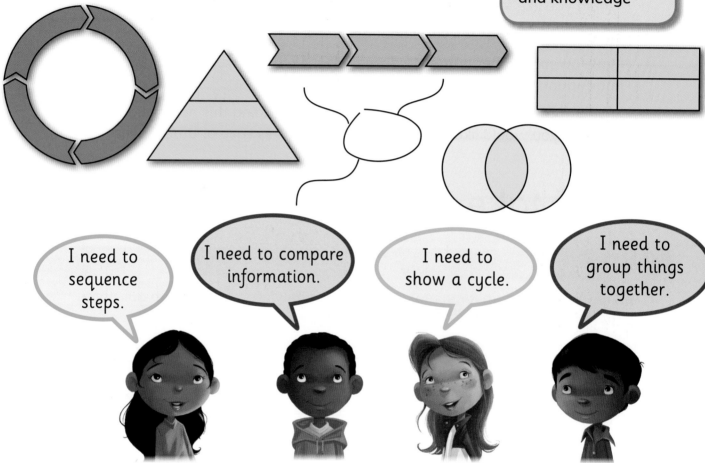

b Which graphic organisers can be used to show the process of how the crystals formed in The Giant Crystal Cave?

c Show how to use it to make notes about this process. Use key words only.

d Write a short summary in your own words explaining how the crystals formed.

Do your notes make sense to you?

Do you need to change how you take notes to make sure they are useful to you?

> 5.9 Recall connectives

We are going to ...

- recall and revise connectives, write a short explanation and self-assess written work.

Getting started

1 A connective is a joining word. Find five connectives in *The Giant Crystal Cave* text in Session 5.7.

2 Discuss the purpose in each case.

1 Recall connectives.

Language focus

Connectives link words, phrases, clauses, sentences and paragraphs.
You can use one or more connectives in a simple sentence. You can use one or more connectives to create multi-clause sentences.

Connectives can show **time and sequence**.	Connectives can show **cause and effect**.	Connectives can **add and compare information**.
later, meanwhile, before, next, after, then, while, first, eventually, recently, when, initially, finally, afterwards	*since, due to, because, so, therefore, thus, consequently, as a result, hence*	*and, as well as, moreover, most of all, not only, also, including, furthermore, similarly, equally, unlike*
<u>After</u> it was discovered, it became famous.	*The cave is dangerous, <u>therefore</u> be careful.*	*<u>Most of all</u>, protect yourself from the heat.*

a Identify three connectives in *The Giant Crystal Cave* text that show:

- time or sequence
- cause and effect
- extra information or comparison

b   Write each sentence into your notebook, <u>underline</u> the connective and say what type it is.

Example: <u>Over time</u>, the hot water filled the cave.
          Time or sequence connective.

- Due to the perfect conditions in the cave, the crystals grew.

- This cave is unique, unlike any other cave known to us.

- Not only is the cave enormous, it is beautiful.

- You must exit the cave after half an hour.

c   Use these sentence starters to write sentences in your notebook to show **cause and effect**.

- The crystals formed because ...

- The cave is dangerous, therefore ...

- As a result, ...

- Wear protective gear since ...

2   Use connectives to explain how to put on the protective gear.

Diagram of the protective gear

Facemask provides chilled air for breathing.

Respirator backpack (20 kg) filled with ice.

Ice vest filled with tubes of iced gel cools the body.

Insulated vest protects the skin and prevents frostbite.

Overalls keep the heat off the ice and provide protection from the sharp crystals.

a   Discuss the photo of protective gear with a partner.
    Work out the sequence of how to put it on.

b   On your own, write a 'How to' heading for your paragraph.

c   Introduce the explanation with a topic sentence like *Visitors must wear the following protective gear.*

d   Explain how to put the gear on in simple, ordered steps – from the first item of clothing.

e   Explain why each item is important.

f   Use connectives of time/sequence and cause/effect to help your paragraph flow and make sense.

    Example: First of all, put on the ... In order to ...

g   Plan your writing and write your first draft, then check and edit it.

h   Write your paragraph out neatly.

How am I doing?

- Have you explained why and how you need to wear protective gear?
- Have you included connectives of time, and cause and effect?
- Is your work well edited and neatly written out or typed?

> 5.10 Explain with multi-clause sentences

We are going to ...

- identify multi-clause sentences, use special connectives and write complex sentences.

Getting started

1   Work with a partner. Find examples in *The Giant Crystal Cave* text in Session 5.7 of simple and multi-clause sentences.

2   Explain the difference between them.

1   Use multi-clause sentences to link information.

Language focus

A **simple sentence** has one clause. A **multi-clause sentence** is formed when you link two or more simple sentences.

A **complex sentence** has a main clause and one or more dependent clauses. The dependent clauses are introduced by the following **special connectives**:

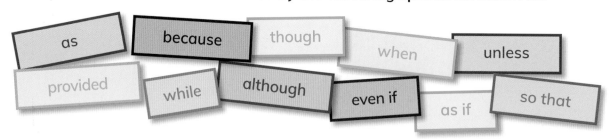

as   because   though   when   unless
provided   while   although   even if   as if   so that

Example: They found the cave **[main clause]** <u>when</u> they were pumping water out of the mine. **[dependent clause]**

If a dependent clause begins a sentence, use a comma to separate it from the main clause.

a Identify two complex sentences in *The Giant Crystal Cave* text.

b Find the main clause in each complex sentence. Write it in your notebook.

- If they are exposed to air, the crystals will deteriorate.
- Giant crystals formed in the cave when it was full of hot water.
- The cave was discovered in 2000 when miners were working there.
- The crystals are dangerous because they are sharp and slippery.
- You won't survive for long inside the cave unless you wear protective gear.

c Now match the main clauses from question **b** with the following dependent clauses. Start each sentence with the main clause. Underline the connective.

Example: The crystals will deteriorate _unless_ scientists can preserve them.

- so you should wear protective gear
- because the conditions were just right
- as water was pumped out of the mine
- although they are very beautiful

d Use the following dependent clauses to begin new sentences. Complete each sentence with your own main clause.

- When you are inside the cave,
- As long as you stay safe,
- Because the crystals are sharp,
- Unless you wear a special suit,

Writing tip

Remember: if you begin a sentence with a dependent clause, use a comma to separate it from the main clause.

e Write two of your own complex sentences about The Giant Crystal Cave.

- Begin the first one with a main clause.
- Begin the second one with a dependent clause.

f Share your sentences in groups. Suggest ways to correct or improve them.

> 5.11 Plan first

We are going to ...

- **listen to a personal account, discuss ideas and plan the layout of an information leaflet.**

Getting started

1 Work in small groups. Describe a place you've visited on holiday.
2 Ask and answer these questions:

Where did you go?

Were you prepared?

What did you do?

Did you forget to pack anything?

1 Talk about visiting The Giant Crystal Cave.

a Listen to an account of what someone experienced inside The Giant Crystal Cave.

b Work together. Discuss the audio. Did that person enjoy his visit to the caves? How do you know? How did he describe it? What facts and details did you hear?

c Imagine visiting the caves. Share ideas. Make notes (on a mind map or table) with headings like:

Glossary

terrain: a particular type of land

impale: push a sharp object through something or someone

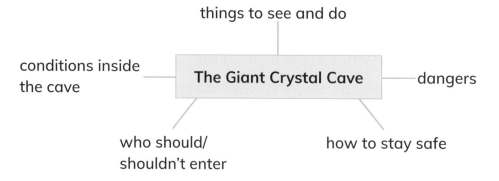

things to see and do

conditions inside the cave

The Giant Crystal Cave

dangers

who should/ shouldn't enter

how to stay safe

d Share your ideas with another group.
Add any extra information to your mind map or table.

2 Plan an adventure leaflet.

a In pairs, plan a leaflet that will inform others about the cave but also explain something.

b Choose the sections you would like in your leaflet.
One section must be an explanation.

c Decide how to set out the information with headings.

d Share your ideas with another pair to check that you are on the right track.

Try arranging your sections and paragraphs in different ways on the page.

Did you plan effectively before you began writing?
How could you make your planning more useful?

> 5.12 Write and present

We are going to ...

- **write a rough draft, check and edit it and present the final version neatly.**

Getting started

Recall differences and similarities between an information text and an explanation.

1 Write a rough draft and then edit it.

  a Use your planning notes to write a first draft of your adventure leaflet with:

  - a heading
  - a topic sentence for each section
  - an impersonal style using third-person pronouns
  - specialised vocabulary
  - facts only (avoid opinions)
  - multi-clause sentences
  - a section to explain how or why with a diagram or picture or map.

  b Check your work. Then swap with a partner and help each other check and suggest ways to improve.

  c Use a dictionary to check and correct spelling.

  d Use a thesaurus to improve your vocabulary.

2 Write it out neatly and present it.

    a Use your notes to write your leaflet out or use on-screen tools to type it.

    b Have someone check it to ensure you haven't left out anything important.

    c Take turns to display and present it to the class. Listen to each other. Afterwards, ask and answer questions to find out more.

    d Read other leaflets and reflect on what works well and looks good.

> **Writing tip**
>
> Presentation is key. Make sure your leaflet looks appealing and is easy to understand.

Look what I can do!

- ☐ I can listen for detail.
- ☐ I can write instructions in order using command verbs and correct pronouns.
- ☐ I can demonstrate in front of an audience.
- ☐ I can summarise and make notes in various ways.
- ☐ I can write an explanation with multi-clause sentences.
- ☐ I can design and edit an information sheet.

Check your progress

1 Identify two textual features of:

An information text   An explanation

2 What type of text is an instruction?

3 Identify the command verbs in the following sentences:

    a Collect the information from various sources.

    b Present the work in an interesting formal.

Continued

4 What is the underlined pronoun referring to in these sentences?

a My friends visited the caves even though <u>they</u> were dangerous.

b I followed the guide's instruction, but <u>it</u> was unclear.

5 Form a multi-clause sentence with the connectives shown in brackets ().

a We visited the cave. It was safe to explore. (as soon as)

b It was hot in the cave. We could not stay long. (because)

6 Identify the dependent clauses in question 5.

Projects

Group project: form an imaginary 'tour guide company'. Choose an interesting, natural landmark in another country that would be fun to visit. Choose different sections to research like: *what it is*, *where it is* (map), *how it formed*, *what to pack* and *how to get there*. Create a travel brochure and information pack for tourists from your research. It can be in leaflet or on-screen form.

Pair project: research different types of caves. Present your research as a table. Include information about what they look like, how they are formed, their locations and how old they are. Use diagrams to illustrate your research.

Solo project: write an imaginative personal account of a time when you visited The Giant Crystal Cave. Include details of what you wore, what you saw and your reactions. Include an illustration of the cave.

6 > A different type of story

> 6.1 The Way Through the Woods

We are going to ...

- skim read a narrative poem, then read it in detail to answer questions.

Getting started

1   Summarise a mystery story you know and tell your partner.

2   Discuss what sort of mystery it is – an unsolved problem, a ghostly event, a detective story or something else?

1 Talk about a mysterious story.

Read *The Way Through the Woods* by the classic poet, Rudyard Kipling.

a Skim the poem for unfamiliar words and check how to pronounce them.

b Now read the poem in detail with a partner.

- Describe the mood of the poem – how does it make you feel?

- How does the poet create this mood?

c What is the mystery in the poem?

2 Unlock the poem's secrets

Discuss the answers to these questions with your partner and then write the answers in your notebook.

a What happened 70 years ago?

b What has happened to the road?

c Who can tell if there was once a road?

d What are the signs of a late summer evening in the woods?

e What will you hear in the woods at that time?

f What is mysterious about hearing this?

g Why do you think the road was closed?

h How do you explain the mystery?

When reading a poem for detail and effect, read it to yourself first and then aloud, to hear the poem as well as read it.

The Way Through the Woods

They shut the road through the woods
Seventy years ago.
Weather and rain have undone it again,
And now you would never know
There was once a road through the woods
Before they planted the trees.
It is underneath the **coppice** and **heath**
And the thin anemones.
Only the keeper sees
That, where the ring-dove **broods**,
And the badgers roll at ease,
There was once a road through the woods.

Yet, if you enter the woods
Of a summer evening late,
When the night-air cools on the trout-ringed pools
Where the otter whistles his mate,
(They fear not men in the woods,
Because they see so few)
You will hear the beat of a horse's feet,
And the swish of a skirt in the dew,
Steadily cantering through
The misty **solitudes**,
As though they perfectly knew
The old lost road through the woods ...
But there is no road through the woods.

Rudyard Kipling

Glossary

coppice: an area of closely planted trees

heath: an area of land where grass and other small plants grow, with few trees or bushes

broods: sits on eggs (birds)

solitudes: places where you are alone without other people

> 6.2 Develop your poetic language

We are going to ...

- **describe and analyse a poem.**

Getting started

1 Explain alliteration to a partner and describe its effect.

2 Give each other examples you can share with the class.

Language focus

Develop your **poetic language.**

full rhyme	word endings sound the same	*flight/sight/white*
half rhyme	*final sounds are similar*	*bold/bald, feel/spill*
internal rhyme	words within a line have a full or half rhyme	*I am the <u>daughter</u> of Earth and <u>Water</u>.*
assonance	words close to each other contain the same vowel sounds	*The <u>girl</u> had <u>pearls</u> on her <u>skirt</u>.*

1 Use words and images to create evocative descriptions.

   a With a partner, discuss the structure of the poem *The Way Through the Woods* in Session 6.1, using the words, *stanzas* and *lines*. Why do you think the poet wrote stanzas of uneven length?

   b • What is described in the first stanza?

      • What is described in the second stanza?

c   In pairs, try to work out the meaning of any unfamiliar <u>words</u>, then check your ideas in a dictionary or online.

d   • What is the effect of the repetition of the word woods?

   • Can you find a half-rhyme for woods in each stanza?

   • What internal rhymes can you find?

   • Can you think of another word to describe these internal rhymes?

Here's a clue – it's one of these: assonance, simile, alliteration.

e   Think of another word to fit each internal rhyme, matching the long, soft vowel sounds.

2   Some words have more than one meaning. Use context to identify the correct one.

a   Which kind of anemone is mentioned in the poem?

anemone n. 1 A type of small plant, wild or grown in gardens, with pink, blue or white flowers. 2 A soft sea creature that looks like a flower and often lives on rocks under the water.

Anemone

Greek anemone (anemone blanda)

wood anemone (anemone nemorosa)

sea anemone

b   What meanings for *keeper* can you find in your dictionary?
Which definition suits the context of the poem best?

c   Why do you think the keeper can tell that there was
once a road through the woods?

d   Which are your favourite lines in the poem? Share
them with another pair explaining why.

e   Summarise the main points of each stanza in one or
two sentences, using expressive words and phrases.

f   Record the poem in your reading log, describing its
mystery and how the writer created the mood.

> **Reading tip**
>
> Words that are spelt
> the same and usually
> sound the same
> but have different
> meanings are called
> *homonyms*.

Would you recognise the different types of rhyme in another poem?

How can you remember the different types?

> 6.3 Bringing the rain

We are going to ...

- **listen and respond to a poem and then compare poems.**

Getting started

1   Tell a partner what you know about Africa.

2   What happens to an area when there is no rain for a long time? Make a list.

1   Listen to the poem.

   a   Listen to your teacher read the poem extract, or listen to the audio recording of it.

   b   How much do you remember after listening?

- Where is the story set?

- What had happened and what was needed?

- Who was there and what was the sequence of events?

   c   Read the poem to yourself to check your answers.

> **Listening tip**
>
> Listen to the poem with your eyes closed and see the images in your head.

Bringing the Rain to Kapiti Plain

This is the great
Kapiti **Plain**,
All fresh and green
from the African rains –
A sea of grass for the
ground birds to nest in,
And patches of shade for
wild creatures to rest in;
With acacia trees for
giraffes to browse on,
And grass for the herdsman
to pasture their cows on.
But one year the rains
were so very **belated**,
That all of the big wild
creatures **migrated**.
Then Ki-pat helped to end
that terrible **drought** –
And this story tells
how it all came about!

This is the cloud,
all heavy with rain,
That shadowed the ground
on Kapiti Plain.

…

This was the shot
that pierced the cloud
and loosed the rain
with thunder LOUD!
A shot from the bow,
so long and strong,
And strung with a string,
a leather thong;
A bow for the arrow
Ki-pat put together,
With a slender stick
and an eagle feather;
From the eagle who happened
to drop a feather,

A feather that helped
to change the weather.
It fell near Ki-pat,
who watched his herd
As he stood on one leg,
like the big stork bird;
Ki-pat, whose cows
were so hungry and dry,
They mooed for the rain
to fall from the sky;
To green up the grass,
all brown and dead,
That needed the rain
from the cloud overhead –
The big, black cloud,
all heavy with rain,
that shadowed the ground
on Kapiti Plain.

Verna Aardema

Glossary

plain: a large area of flat land

belated: delayed

migrated: travelled to a different place, usually when the season changes (animals)

drought: a long period when there is little or no rain

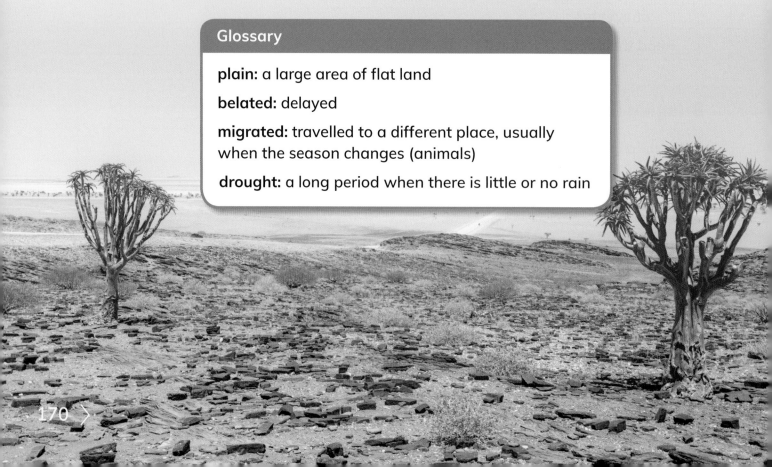

2 Analyse the writer's techniques with a partner.

   a Describe the poem's structure in terms of stanzas, lines, punctuation and sentences.

   b Identify the poetic techniques the writer has used, giving examples.

rhyme   rhythm   repetition   imagery   text effects   narrative voice (who is telling the story)   figurative language   language and word choice

   c • How is the grass described for the ground birds to nest in?

   • Is this a literal or a figurative description? How can you tell?

   • What is this type of description called – when you say something <u>is</u> something else?

   d • Find a simile in the poem.

   • Do you think it is an effective simile?
     What picture do you have of how Ki-pat is standing?

   e How do you think the poem continues?

3 Compare one poem with another.

a Practise your technique for reading a poem with understanding.

> **Reading tip**
>
> Look at the layout of the poem 'Once the Wind' and think about how it adds to the overall effect of the poem.

Once the Wind

Once the wind
said to the sea
I am sad
   And the sea said
Why
   And the wind said
Because I
am not blue like the sky
or like you

   So the sea said what's
so sad about that
   Lots
of things are blue
or red or other colours too
but nothing

neither sea nor sky
can blow as strong
or sing so long as you

And the sea looked sad
   So the wind said
Why

Shake Keane
(St Vincent, West Indies)

b Who is the conversation between?

c Predict what the wind might have said to cheer up the sea.

d What poetic technique is used to describe the sea and the wind?

e Compare the structure and language of *Bringing the Rain to Kapiti Plain* and *Once the Wind*.

- Talk about stanzas, lines, punctuation, sentences and dialogue.

- Talk about poetic techniques, such as rhyme, rhythm, figurative language and imagery, repetition, narrative voice and language style.

f Record your reading of the two poems in your reading log, explaining which one you preferred and why.

How am I doing?

- Were you able to compare the structure of the poems?

- Were you able to compare and contrast the poetic techniques?

> 6.4 Read with understanding

We are going to ...

- **read a poem with understanding before performing it in a group.**

Getting started

1 In the poem *Once the Wind*, imagine the sky joined in the wind and sea's conversation.

2 Why might the sky have been sad? What could the others have said to cheer up the sky?

1 Find the evidence

Bringing the Rain to Kapiti Plain

a How did Ki-Pat help bring the rain?

b Can this really be done? Explain.

c Put the sequence of events in a timeline.

d Describe the mood in the poem – how does it make you feel?

e How has the writer achieved this effect?

Reading tip

Abstract nouns name things we experience but cannot touch like ideas and feelings.

Once the Wind

f Explain how you can read the poem expressively even though it has no punctuation.

g Write out the poem in your notebook in sentences and paragraphs. Add the punctuation you think should be there – including for the dialogue.

h Describe the mood in the poem – how does it make you feel?

i How has the writer achieved this effect?

2 Perform one of the poems.

a Make notes to plan how to read one of the poems as a group.

- Which parts could be read by a single voice and which as a group?

- What sound effects or actions could add to the effect?

b Practise reading the poem. Learn your lines by heart for added fluency. How does it sound? Does it capture the mood?

c Perform the poem for the class.

How are we doing?

- Did the group capture the mood of the poem in their reading?

- Did each person perform fluently and confidently using performance techniques?

⟩ 6.5 Not lost but found

We are going to ...

- read a narrative poem, analysing writing techniques and figures of speech.

Getting started

1   Talk to a partner about what happens to you at the end of a school day.

2   How do you get home? Who comes to fetch you? What do you take with you?

1   Read *At the End of a School Day*.

   a   How do you feel at the end of a school day?
        Think about the sounds, actions and atmosphere.

   b   Summarise the end of your school day in a mind map of words and phrases.
        Use a thesaurus to help you choose descriptive words.

   c   Read *At the End of a School Day* together and compare it with the mood
        at the end of your school day.

At the End of a School Day

1   It is the end of a school day
     and down the long drive
     come bag-swinging, shouting children.

2   Deafened, the sky **winces**.

3   The sun gapes in surprise.

4   Suddenly the runners skid to a stop,
     stand still and stare
     at a small hedgehog
     curled-up on the **tarmac**
     like an old, frayed cricket ball.

5   A girl dumps her bag, tiptoes forward
     and gingerly, so **gingerly**
     carries the creature
     to the safety of a shady hedge.

6   Then steps back, watching.

7   Girl, children, sky and sun
     hold their breath.

8   There is a silence,
     a moment to remember
     on this warm afternoon in June.

Wes Magee

Glossary

winces: shows pain or embarrassment, suddenly and for a short time, in the face

tarmac: black material used for building roads, etc., consisting of tar mixed with small stones

gingerly: in a careful, cautious way

d   Discuss the story in the poem with your partner.

- Why do the runners stop?
- Why does the girl move the hedgehog?
- What adverb is used to describe how she moves it?
- What does this adverb mean? Use the context to help you.
- Find two synonyms for this adverb.

e   Why do you think everyone and everything hold their breath?

f   What is the *moment to remember*? Summarise it in a sentence.

Language focus

Figures of speech recap

Similes use *like* or *as* to compare things.

His hands were <u>as</u> cold <u>as</u> ice. The flower was <u>like</u> a jewel.

Metaphors say one thing is another thing.

The road was a snake slithering up the hill.

Personification gives a non-living thing human characteristics.

The moon took fright as day crept forward.

2   The poet uses figurative language, including personification.

a   What figure of speech is used to describe the hedgehog?

b   Make up another comparison of this type and share it with a partner.

c   Which two objects are personified in the first stanza (column 1), and how?

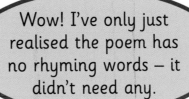

d
- Who holds their breath in the second stanza (column 2)?
- What picture does this conjure up in your head?
- Why is it such an effective image?

3 Other writing techniques.

a Is this poem in first- or third-person narrative? Which words tell you this?

b How would the poem change with a different narrative person?

c
- What is the tense of the poem?
- What effect does this have on the action in the story?

d What is the effect of sentences 2 and 3, coming after the longer first sentence?

e What is unsettling about sentence 6? Why do you think the poet did this?

Writing tip

Simple sentences express one idea with <u>one complete verb</u> – called a finite verb.

Compound or complex sentences often express more than one main idea, with <u>more than one complete verb,</u> and often with more than one subject.

---

f How many complete verbs are in sentences 4 and 5?

g
- Sentences 4 and 5 have lists with commas. What is being listed?
- Find another list with commas in the poem.

> Wow! I've only just realised the poem has no rhyming words – it didn't need any.

h
- How many complete or finite verbs does sentence 8 have?
- What is the purpose of the comma in sentence 8?

i Update your reading log and record what figurative language was used.

> 6.6 Use a frame to write a poem

We are going to ...

- plan and write a poem using a frame.

Getting started

Work with a partner and give each other ideas for personification for these non-living things: *a school, a car, a shop, and the wind.*

1   Use a frame to plan.

   a   Decide on a story about finding an unusual thing in a familiar place.

   b   Follow the format of *At the End of a School Day* to plan your poem.

Sentence 1	set the scene
Sentence 2	one-line, simple sentence with personification
Sentence 3	one-line, simple sentence with personification
Sentence 4	longer sentence with three finite verbs in list format; build up to the complication with a simile
Sentence 5	longer sentence with three finite verbs in list format; build up to the climax
Sentence 6	simple, one-line sentence emphasising the build-up
Sentence 7	simple sentence creating the drama of the climax
Sentence 8	simple sentence expressing a final, thoughtful reflection

2   Write without stopping.

   a   Write your poem's first draft in the present tense to create immediacy.

   b   Make sure every word counts. Use a thesaurus or your own list of words to help you choose effective adjectives, adverbs and descriptive language.

   c   Ask your partner to read your poem aloud. How does it sound? Does it flow and create the mood and drama that you want?

   d   Make changes to improve it and to edit and proofread it, using different strategies to work out spellings before using a dictionary.

3   Read out each other's poems.

   a   Swap and read each other's poems aloud in a group. Does your poem sound how you expected? Give reasons.

   b   Say what you liked about how your poem was read out, and what you enjoyed about the other poems you heard.

Speaking tip

Read your partner's poem to yourself several times before reading it aloud.

Did your poem sound how you expected?

How did it sound different from what you imagined?

179

Look what I can do!

☐ I can listen, read, respond to and compare poems.

☐ I can talk about a poem using poetic language.

☐ I can identify and analyse poetic techniques.

☐ I can answer questions using evidence from the poem.

☐ I can perform a poem with expression and meaning.

☐ I can plan and write a poem using a frame.

Check your progress

1 Write two ways a poet can create a mood of mystery in a poem.

2 Organise these words into pairs in a table with columns for *full rhyme* and *half rhyme*:

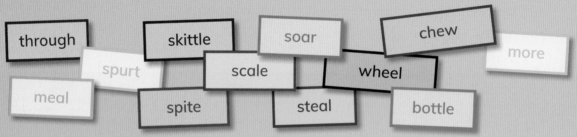

Full rhyme	Half rhyme

3 Describe the rhyming pattern in 'Bringing the Rain to Kapiti Plain' in Session 6.3. Use letters to show the pattern in the first eight lines, for example AABB.

4 • Give an example of personification for a fridge.

 • Give a metaphor for a fridge.

 • Give a simile for a fridge.

5 Use a thesaurus or your own knowledge to write two synonyms for each adverb:

Projects

Group project: perform the poems you wrote in the final session. Bring the performances to life with sound effects, props, music and choral and solo recitals.

Pair project: create a poster to illustrate and advertise a performance of the poems you wrote in the final session. Include the titles, themes and text to persuade people to come to listen, as well as illustrations.

Solo project: research poetry anthologies, books and online to find examples of narrative poetry – poetry that tells a story. Draw up a table of poems, including source, title, author and theme.

> 7.1 Fairy tales forever

We are going to …

- read, summarise and explore the features of fairy tales.

Getting started

1   Explain to a partner what a fairy tale is.

2   Give each other examples of ones that you know.

1   Read the following fairy story and discuss the questions in a group.

The Salt Prince

Once upon a time in a kingdom far away, there lived a king and his three sons. One day, eager to know who loved him the most, the king asked them, "How much do you love me?"

The eldest replied, "I love you more than gold!" The king was delighted.

The second son replied, "I love you more than diamonds!" The king was elated.

The youngest replied, "I love you more than salt!" The king was furious. More than salt? How dare he compare his love with something of such low value? In his rage, he **banished** his youngest son from the kingdom. He left, taking with him all the salt in the land.

Soon afterwards, the king's appetite began to **wane**, for the food no longer tasted good. Without nourishment, he became weak and ill, but nothing could tempt him to eat. He could no longer take pleasure in either his food or his life. As he lay dying, his youngest son returned, bringing with him a dish of warm, salty **broth**. With the first delicious taste, the king felt his strength and his **relish** for life begin to return.

He realised at last that his youngest son loved him most of all, for when he had said he loved him more than salt, he meant he loved him more than that which sustains life, and more than the joy of life itself. And that is a great love indeed.

a   Retell the story to a partner in your own words.

b   How did the king react when his son compared his love to salt? Why?

c   How do you think you would have reacted?

d   Why did the king become so ill?

e   How did he get better?

f   What did the king realise at the end?

g   Is this story real? How can you tell?

h   What facts are there in the story about table salt?

> **Glossary**
>
> **banished:** sent someone away from a place, often as a punishment
>
> **wane:** reduce or shrink
>
> **broth:** a thin soup of meat, fish or vegetable stock
>
> **relish:** enjoyment or enthusiasm for something

Add the story to your reading log and comment on how it is similar to or different from other fairy tales you know.

2   What makes a fairy tale?

a   How many of these fairy tales do you know?

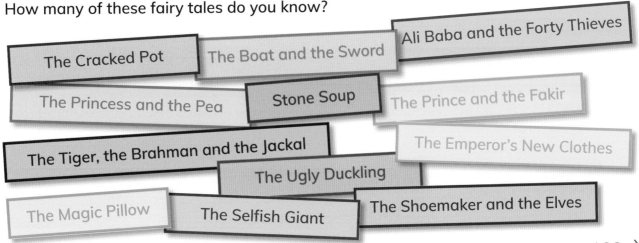

The Cracked Pot · The Boat and the Sword · Ali Baba and the Forty Thieves · The Princess and the Pea · Stone Soup · The Prince and the Fakir · The Tiger, the Brahman and the Jackal · The Emperor's New Clothes · The Ugly Duckling · The Magic Pillow · The Selfish Giant · The Shoemaker and the Elves b   Create a mind map of other fairy tales you know, including fairy stories or traditional tales from your region. Use key details only.

c   Summarise one of the stories to a partner.

> **Speaking tip**
>
> When you summarise the story, focus on main characters and events – leave out the detail.

d   Do your stories have any similar introductions, characters, themes, events or endings?

e   Share your stories with another pair.
    Which traditional tale features do they share?

- unlikely events
- a timeless setting (Once upon a time)
- enchanted objects
- wicked stepmothers or stepsisters
- a good nature triumphing over greed, foolishness, selfishness or wickedness
- kings, queens, princes and princesses

- a task or test
- cleverness or wisdom rewarded
- three people/events/wishes/ challenges
- themes, e.g. good–evil, poor–rich, generous–selfish, foolish–wise
- transformation, e.g. rags to riches, proud to humble, greedy to generous, foolish to wise.

f   Which traditional tale features does *The Salt Prince* have?

Did the mind map help you to compare features?
Would a different method be more useful for you?

> 7.2 A well-known tale around the world

We are going to ...

- **read and listen to a synopsis and compare different story versions.**

Getting started

1 Have you ever seen a play or a film version of a fairy tale or a traditional tale?

2 Describe it to a partner. Was it different or faithful to the original tale?

1 Some fairy tales have been retold around the world for centuries.

    a In a group, read the synopsis of this traditional Persian tale. What other fairy tales does it remind you of?

    b What is similar and what is different?

    c What traditional features does this tale have?

Today, Persia is called Iran. Do you know any other countries that have changed their names?

Synopsis of Persian tale

Settareh has to do all the **chores** for her stepmother and wears her stepsisters' old clothes. Jealous of her beauty and good nature, they mock her rags until she feels ashamed. Meanwhile, the king invites everyone to the New Year, No Ruz, celebration. Instead of buying a dress, Settareh spends her money on others in need and an unusual blue jug, which turns out to be enchanted. She wishes for a beautiful gown for No Ruz. At the celebration, she meets a handsome prince but has to **flee** dramatically to avoid her stepmother and in so doing loses her **anklet**.

The prince eventually finds Settareh, but her jealous sisters find the jug and wish to be rid of her. Six jewelled hairpins appear which they pin into Settareh's hair, turning her into a turtledove. Although the prince thinks he has lost her, Settareh, the bird, sings to him each evening. One night, he sees the pins, pulls them out and so sets Settareh free. They live happily ever after.

Key word

synopsis: a short description of the contents of something such as a book or film

Glossary

chores: a job or piece of work that is often boring or unpleasant but needs to be done regularly

flee: escape by running away, especially because of danger or fear

anklet: a chain or ring worn as jewellery around the ankle

2   Compare different versions of the story.

a   Listen to your teacher read a synopsis of *Cinderella* or listen to the audio recording of it.

Listening tip

Listen to how the readers use expression to add drama to the story.

- How does it compare with other versions of *Cinderella* that you know?

- If you have seen a film, play or other version, how does it compare with that?

b Answer these questions on the story.

- Why does the king invite all unmarried girls to the palace?

- Why does the fairy godmother warn Cinderella to be home by midnight?

- Why does the prince search for the glass slipper's owner?

- What sort of ending does the story have?

c How does it compare to the Persian version of the tale?
Draw up a table of similarities and differences.

Similarities	Differences
They both have stepmothers and stepsisters. ...	

The Disney film of *Cinderella* is based on a 17th-century French version of the story called *The Little Glass Slipper* by Charles Perrault.

How are we doing?

Can you identify the features of a fairy tale?
Can you compare two versions of the same story?

> 7.3 Compare and contrast

We are going to ...

- answer questions on synopses and prepare a report.

Getting started

1   How could the *Cinderella* tale be adapted for your region?

2   Discuss ideas with a partner.

1   Explore different versions of the *Cinderella* tale.

   a   Skim read the *Cinderella* synopses from China and Kenya. Have you heard these versions or other versions in your region?

   b   How are they similar to or different from the *Cinderella* and *Settareh* stories? Tell your partner.

   c   Add the *Cinderella* synopses to your reading log. Which one do you prefer?

Speaking tip

Break down unfamiliar names into syllables to help you pronounce them:

Set/tah/reh

Yeh-/Shen

Chin/ye

Synopsis of *Cinderella* in China

Tuan Ch'eng-shih wrote the earliest known version of Cinderella *in the mid-9th century.* Yeh-Shen's stepmother treats her harshly. Her only friend is a magical fish in the river. One day, her stepmother catches the fish and cooks it for supper. An old man tells the miserable Yeh-Shen to keep the fish bones and make a wish when she really needs something. When she wishes to be able to attend the Spring Festival, her clothes are transformed into an **exotic** outfit with golden slippers. Yeh-Shen loses one golden slipper while fleeing her stepmother at the festival. The king searches for its owner. The king's men catch Yeh-Shen creeping in to reclaim her slipper and bring her before the king. When she puts it on, her beautiful festival outfit reappears. The king falls in love with Yeh-Shen and they marry.

Synopsis of *Cinderella* in Kenya

Chinye's cruel stepmother sends her into the night forest to fetch water but instead of attacking her, the animals keep her safe. On her return, Chinye meets an old woman who asks her to sweep her hut. She tells Chinye to take the tiniest, quietest **gourd** from the floor and break it open at home. When Chinye does so, treasure spills out of the gourd. Her greedy stepsister dashes off to find the old woman's hut, but instead of sweeping the floor and taking the tiniest gourd, she grabs the largest and scurries home. Instead of treasure, a swarm of vicious wasps bursts out, forcing the stepmother and stepsister to flee. Chinye is alone, but instead of spending her wealth on herself, she invites the village women to share it and build a **thriving** community.

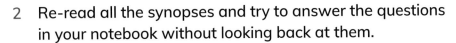

2   Re-read all the synopses and try to answer the questions in your notebook without looking back at them.

Glossary

exotic: unusual, interesting and often foreign

gourd: a large fruit that has a hard shell and cannot be eaten, or the shell of this fruit used as a container

thriving: growing, developing or being successful

a   **Persia**

- How do Settareh's stepsisters make her feel ashamed?
- What does Settareh do instead of buying a dress?
- What does this tell you about her nature?
- How do the sisters show they are more jealous than ever?
- How does Settareh show her loyalty and how is it rewarded?

b   **China**

- Who is Yeh-Shen's only friend?
- Why do you think this is?
- What does Yeh-Shen wish for and how is her wish answered?
- Why do you think Yeh-Shen's wish is granted?

c **Kenya**

- How can you tell that Chinye's stepmother does not care for her?

- Why do you think the animals protect Chinye?

- How is Chinye's life transformed in the story?

- What does Chinye do instead of falling in love with a prince or king?

How are we doing?

Swap notebooks with a partner and check each other's answers.

3 Which key *Cinderella* elements appear in the different versions of the tale?

a In pairs, draw up a table of key *Cinderella* features and tick which of the stories share each element.

Cinderella story element	Yeh-Shen	Chinye	Settareh
Wicked or cruel stepmother	✓	✓	✓

b Prepare a short oral report on the different versions of the story.

c • Introduce the report, explaining what it is about.

- Explain how two or three key elements from your table differ or are similar.

- Finish by saying which version you prefer and why.

d Present your report to another pair or another class and listen to their questions and feedback.

> 7.4 Phrases, clauses and tenses

We are going to ...

- **work with phrases, clauses, connectives and the present tense.**

Getting started

1   Use the verb to be in the past, present and futures tenses in sentences.

2   Do the same with the verb to have.

1   Phrases and clauses add variety and detail to sentences

Language focus

Phrases are groups of words that work together and which **do not contain a verb.**

Phrases can do the job of:

- adjectives: *The girl <u>with ragged, dirty clothes</u>.*

- adverbs: *She swept the floor <u>with energy and enthusiasm</u>.*

Clauses are groups of words that work together and which **do contain a verb.**

Clauses can do the job of:

- adjectives: *The girl <u>who **had** braids in her hair</u>.*

- adverbs: *She swept the floor <u>while she **sang** to herself</u>.*

Adverbial clauses say when, where or how the action happened.

a   Decide if the <u>underlined</u> words are phrases or clauses.

- <u>With an evil gleam in her eyes</u>, her stepmother cooked Yeh-Shen's fish.

- <u>After Chinye finished her work</u>, her stepmother sent her into the woods.

- Yeh-Shen <u>in her new clothes</u> gasped <u>with a cry of delight</u>.

- Settareh bought a blue jug <u>that had flowers around the rim.</u>

- <u>As the clock struck midnight,</u> Cinderella ran <u>like the wind</u>.

b Identify the verbs and then write down the connective that joins the clauses together.

- Chinye was anxious when her mother sent her into the woods.

- Before she went to the Spring Festival, Yeh-Shen's clothes were transformed into an exotic outfit.

- Settareh sings to the prince every night while he searches for her.

- After she swept her floor, the old woman gave Chinye a gourd.

- When she found out about the magic fish, Yeh-Shen's stepmother caught and ate the fish.

> ### Writing tip
>
> Connectives that join clauses are sometimes placed at the start of a sentence, with the clauses separated by a comma to clarify meaning.

c Decide which clause is the main clause and which is the adverbial clause in the sentences in question **b**.

d Write down the purpose of each adverbial clause in 1 b (e.g. how, when or where).

2   Fairy stories are often set *long, long ago* or *once upon a time*.

Language focus

There are two forms of the **present tense**.

- The **simple form** shows things are done repeatedly. It shows it has been done before and is likely to be done again.

    Example: Chinye <u>cleans</u> the house every day.
    Yeh-Shen <u>visits</u> her fish in the morning.

- The **longer form** indicates something is happening **right now**. The verb is formed from a helping verb and the present participle of the main verb (e.g. *fishing, cleaning, speaking, smiling*).

    Settareh is singing to the prince.

    subject   helping verb   present participle

    Her sisters are sticking hairpins into her.

---

a   What tense is a story usually written in?

b   • What tense is used in each synopsis? What is the effect?

   • In pairs, each read one synopsis to the other, one partner changing the story into the past tense and the other into the future tense.

   • How does the tense change the effect of the story?

c   Choose the correct form of the verb *to be* to make these sentences happen right now.

   Example: Yeh-Shen (*to be*) *is feeding* her friend the fish.

   • Settareh's sisters (*to be*) *teasing* her again.

   • While Settareh (*to be*) *singing*, the prince spots the pins.

- The animals (to be) protecting Chinye from harm.
- 'Why (to be) you crying?' asked the old man.

d   Write down the root verb in each of the sentences in question **e**.

Example: *feeding → feed*

e   Choose a suitable present participle to complete these sentences:

Example: The prince is (~~verb~~) searching for Settareh.

- The gourds are all (verb) to be picked up by Chinye.
- Why is Yeh-Shen (verb) from the festival?
- What are you (verb) for No Ruz this year?
- We are (verb) the king will notice us at the festival.

> 7.5 and 7.6 Write a synopsis

We are going to …

- **plan, write and edit a synopsis in pairs.**

Getting started

1   What would it be like if the Cinderella character in the stories was a boy, or if the stories were set in modern times?

2   Discuss how the *Cinderella* story might change with a partner.

1   The *Cinderella* story still inspires books and films today.
    Each new version adds fresh ideas to make it original and different.

    a   In pairs, discuss ideas for a *Cinderella* story.

        • What will the Cinderella character be like?

        • Who will the other main characters be?

        • Who or what will the helping character or thing be?

        • Where will it be set? What **local colour** will you
          include (such as clothing, way of life or culture)?

        • What will be the climax and resolution?

> **Glossary**
>
> **local colour:** details that are special and particular to your region

    b   Use a flow chart to plan the story with key words and phrases:

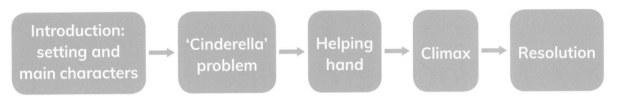

Introduction: setting and main characters → 'Cinderella' problem → Helping hand → Climax → Resolution

    Include local colour from where you live.

2   Write and edit your synopsis.

    a   Together, in pairs, write a synopsis of the story.

        • Use the present tense.

        • Use the third-person narrative.

        • Use simple and multi-clause sentences.

        • Use descriptive phrases and clauses
          to add interest.

        • Use words from your word list of
          words you would like to use again.

    b   Review and edit your synopsis to make
        sure it flows, covers the key elements
        of your story and includes some
        local colour.

    c   Read your synopsis to another pair.
        Ask questions and comment on each
        other's stories.

d   Make improvements to your synopsis based on the feedback received.

e   Proofread your synopsis carefully for tenses, spelling, grammar and punctuation.

How are we doing?

- Did we include only the key points of the story?
- Did we write consistently in the present tense, using the third-person narrative?
- Did we include local colour?

Writing tip

Add any words you mis-spelt/learnt to your spelling log so you know what you need to learn.

> 7.7 Blackberry Blue

We are going to ...

- read, analyse and explore the features and descriptive language of a text.

Getting started

1   Explain the features of a fairy tale to a partner.

2   Give each other examples from fairy tales that you know.

1   *Blackberry Blue* is a fairy tale written by Jamila Gavin.

a   Read and discuss the extract from *Blackberry Blue* with a partner.

- What elements of a fairy tale does it have?
- What do you think will happen when Blackberry Blue grows up?

Blackberry Blue

1   This king thought he was the happiest man alive. His queen, whom he loved so dearly, gave birth to a son. Now he had an heir to take the throne, and the whole kingdom rejoiced. The baby prince was called Just. But even before the celebrations had ended, the young queen died, and the king was heartbroken.

2   In the forests where he often went hunting lived a woodcutter and his wife. They longed for a child, but the years went by and no baby was born to them.

One day, the woodcutter's wife goes into the woods searching for blackberries. She got a little bit lost, lay down and fell asleep.

3   It was a cry that woke the woodcutter's wife: a thin, **plaintive**, hungry cry; a sad, abandoned baby's cry. She sat up with a shiver. Everything was deathly still. All she could hear was the sharp, clipped caws of the rooks, and the high-pitched squeak of bats. The baby's cry had been a dream, she reassured herself.

4   She scrambled to her feet, feeling wobbly and chilled to the bone. She scooped up her basket, ready to go home, when she saw a huge rambling, shambling, prickly, thorny wall of brambles, positively glistening with the fattest, juiciest blackberries she had ever seen.

5   The woodcutter's wife rushed forward. How could she have missed it? She began to pick as fast as she could; so fast that the thorns pricked her fingers and tore at her arms, and her blood ran into the juice. There seemed no end to the **profusion** of blackberries, and soon her basket was full to the brim. Her fingers were quite purple, her legs were scratched, and her skirts were all tangled in the thorns. When at last she tried to scramble out, she found that she was trapped.

6   She struggled this way and that in her efforts to get free, but seemed to be **caught fast**. She was beginning to despair when she heard a faint cry. It was the same sound which had awoken her from her dream: a thin, plaintive, hungry cry; a sad, abandoned baby's cry.

Glossary

plaintive: sounding sad

profusion: an extremely large amount of something

caught fast: stuck

And there, right in the very middle of the prickles **and blackberries,** cradled in the briar, was a tiny little **baby girl.**

7 "Good heavens!" exclaimed the woman. "What's this?" She pushed her way deeper into the thorns.

8 And there, right in the very middle of the prickles and blackberries, cradled in the briar, was a tiny little baby girl.

9 Her skin was as black as midnight, her lips like crushed **damsons**, and her tightly curled hair shone like threads of black gold. When the baby looked up into the woman's face, her eyes glistened like blackberries.

10 "Oh my goodness!" exclaimed the woodcutter's wife. "You poor little thing!" And she scooped up the infant and popped her into her large apron pocket. Miraculously, the thorns didn't scratch her as she turned to find a way out, and the brambles seemed to part as she backed, unhindered, into the open. Although she looked about her and even called out, no one appeared to claim the child. "Well, my little berry, I'll just have to take you home," she murmured.

11 The woodcutter and his wife loved their **foundling** child, and named her Blackberry Blue.

12 The years went by, and Blackberry Blue grew into the most beautiful girl anyone had ever seen. The woodcutter enjoyed making wooden toys for his little daughter, and the woodcutter's wife loved plaiting her black curls, and twisting them with acorns and leaves, and Blackberry Blue grew up the happiest of children; so loved and **nurtured**, becoming more lovely with every day that passed.

Jamila Gavin

Glossary

damsons: sour, dark blue fruits of a type of plum tree

foundling: a young child left by its parents and then found and cared for by someone else

nurtured: taken care of, fed, and protected, especially young children or plants

b   Make a table of fairy tale features in your notebook – you will add to it later as well.

Fairy tale feature	Example from text
Kings, queens, princes and princesses	The king and queen have a son – Prince Just

c   Predict what you think might happen in this fairy tale, using your knowledge of fairy tale features.

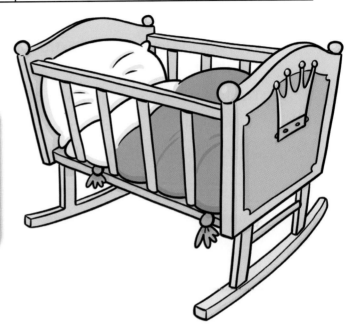

Reading tip

When you make a prediction, use clues from the text, your own knowledge of fairy tale features and your imagination.

2   Authors choose words and layout carefully for effect.

a   • List the words that describe the cry that woke the woodcutter's wife in paragraph 3. List them in alphabetical order.

    • Use a thesaurus and find a synonym for each adjective.

    • Write out the description with your new adjectives. Does it have the same effect?

b   • Find a list of adjectives describing brambles and write out the sentence in your notebook.

    • Underneath the sentence, draw what you think the brambles look like.

c   Find a paragraph with four similes in it. List them in your notebook and add two more similes of your own to the list. How do they add to the effect?

d • Scan the text for interesting adjectives and verbs that you would like to use again.

• Write the words you have chosen in your wordbook.

• Use a thesaurus and add synonyms to your words.

e How did the layout and illustrations add to the effect?

f Think about the paragraphs in the extract.

• Why did the author start a new paragraph each time?

• What is the effect of the different-length paragraphs?

Could the synonyms replace the words in the text and have the same effect?

Did you notice the descriptive language in the text?
How could you make your own descriptions more powerful?

> 7.8 Pronouns, homophones and homonyms

We are going to ...

• explore possessive pronouns and adjectives, as well as homonyms.

Getting started

1 Explain to a partner why we use pronouns in writing.

2 How could you make this sentence flow better?

Blackberry Blue gave one of Blackberry Blue's pies to the prince Blackberry Blue met on the road.

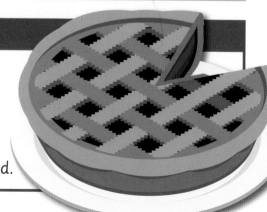

1   Pronouns stand in for nouns to help avoid repetition, but it's important to be clear which noun the pronoun is standing in for.

Personal pronouns	Possessive pronouns	Possessive adjectives
I, you, he, she, it, we, they	*mine, yours, his, hers, ours, theirs*	*my, your, his, her, its, our, their*

a   In the following sentence, whose slippers is Suri's sister wearing?

Suri asked her sister whether the slippers she was wearing were hers.

b   Explain the ambiguity in these sentences.

- Jerome won't play chess with his brother because he always wins.

- As Lily took her book out of her bag, she dropped it.

- The bus crashed into the gate but it wasn't damaged.

c   Suggest ways to make the meanings clear.

> **Key word**
>
> ambiguity: having more than one possible meaning and possibly causing confusion

2   Possessive adjectives (linked to possessive pronouns) or determiners can also be ambiguous.

a   What is ambiguous about these sentences?

- Rafael visited Ahmed after <u>his</u> birthday.

- The teacher gave the learner <u>her</u> pen.

- Indira's friend and <u>her</u> mother came to tea.

b   Suggest ways to make the meanings clear.

c   Are the <u>underlined</u> words adjectives or pronouns?

- I lost my coat, so the prince gave me <u>his</u>.

- We gave <u>our</u> opinion of the story.

- The old woman bent down to pick up <u>her</u> broom.

- That idea was <u>mine</u>.

- <u>Their</u> answer was that the ball was <u>theirs</u>.

> Adjectives modify or describe a noun; pronouns are used in place of a noun.

3 Homophones and homonyms can be confusing too

Language focus

Homophones are words that sound similar but have different spellings and meanings.

their (possessive adjective)

there (adverb of place)

they're (contraction of they are)

Homonyms are words that usually sound the same and are spelt the same but have different meanings.

bow 1 n. knot with two curved parts and two loose ends, used to tie shoes or as decoration

2 n. long, thin piece of wood with hair stretched between the ends, used to play some musical instruments

3 n. piece of curved wood with string fixed to both ends, used for shooting arrows.

---

a Use *their, there* or *they're* to complete each sentence correctly.

- What happened to _____ shoes?

- Do you want me to stand here or _____?

- If _____ ready, they can begin walking.

- I will prepare _____ lunch before I go.

- When _____ ready, we can watch them perform.

- We saw him over _____ under the balcony.

b Look up each of these homonyms in the dictionary and make up a sentence of your own for each meaning you find.

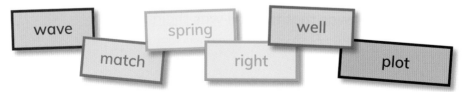

wave   spring   well   match   right   plot

> 7.9 More about Blackberry Blue

We are going to ...

- predict how a story ends and give a group presentation.

Getting started

1   Look up the meaning of *just* in a dictionary.

2   Which meaning do you think applies to Prince Just's name?

3   Why do you think he was called this?

1   Read a story retelling.

   a   Read Nazim's recount of the *Blackberry Blue* tale.
       He has left out the story's ending.

   b   What fairy tale does it remind you of? Give reasons.

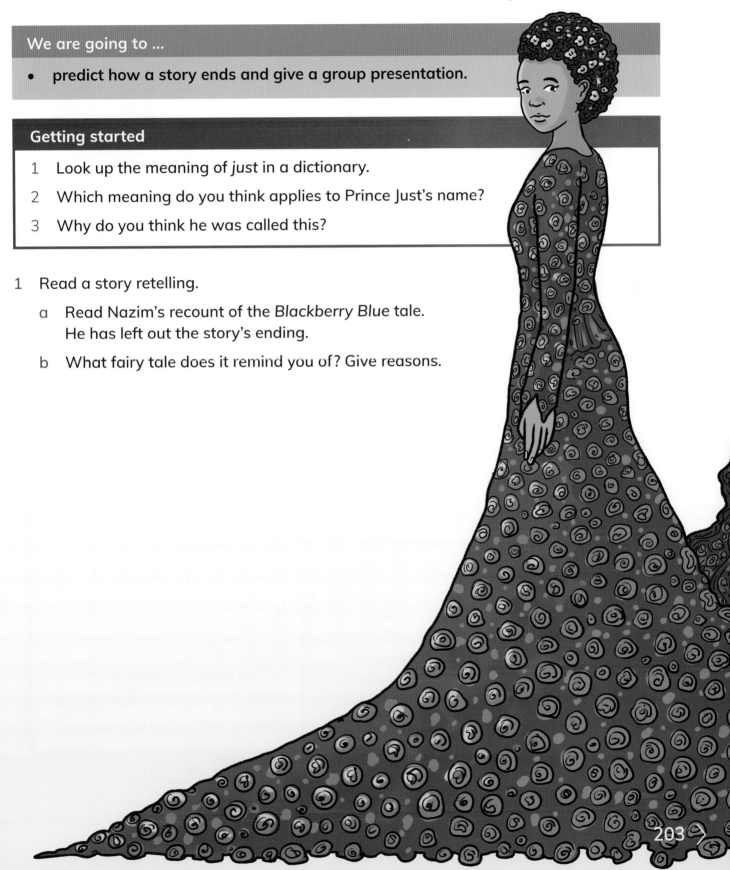

From a retelling of *Blackberry Blue*

After the woodcutter and his wife died, Blackberry Blue went to the brambly bush where she was found as a baby. As she was weeping there, she heard a voice telling her to make a **cloak** of brambles to always keep her safe. She knew it was somehow her real mother's voice. The next autumn she visited the bush again and the voice told her to go to the castle to bake her blackberry pies but to **beware** of the cruel queen. After Prince Just's mother died, the king had married again. He had married a beautiful queen with her own son, Prince Wolf. Although she was beautiful, people **gossiped** that she was evil as rooms grew chill when she entered and flowers died.

Some years earlier, Prince Just had met Blackberry Blue while he was riding with his stepbrother, Prince Wolf, and had bought one of her pies. He had never forgotten her beauty. Every year, the Spring Ball was held to which every girl in the land was invited, hoping that the two princes would find wives. Prince Just was hopeful that he would see Blackberry Blue at the ball as he had fallen in love with her just as she had fallen in love with him. Blackberry Blue's brambly mother made her a dress of spring flowers and every head turned to stare as she arrived as her beauty was like blossom in spring. But every time Prince Just tried to dance with her, Prince Wolf would whirl her away to spite him, as he always did.

As dawn approached, Blackberry Blue fled knowing her dress would wither away. Summer came and another ball and once more Blackberry Blue's brambly mother made her a dress, this time of summer flowers. Again, Prince Wolf dragged Blackberry Blue to dance to **taunt** his stepbrother and at dawn, once more she fled. Prince Just followed the trail of petals to no avail. On his return, he was attacked by a grey, snarling wolf who left him for dead. Blackberry Blue found and tended to Prince Just, moving him to where he would be found.

Prince Just was ill for many months, up until the Autumn Ball. Blackberry Blue started taking him her blackberry pies and warned him not to drink the soup as she feared the queen was poisoning it. On the day of the ball, Blackberry Blue had a dress of autumn leaves with red berries and white winter roses. Once more Prince Wolf had grabbed her hand when Prince Just suddenly appeared at the ball, miraculously cured, **vowing** to marry the girl who had saved his life both in the woods and in the castle ...

Glossary

cloak: a loose coat without sleeves that hangs down from your shoulders

beware: be on one's guard

gossiped: talked about other people's private lives

taunt: repeatedly say or do unkind things to someone to upset them or make them angry

vowing: promising or pledging

c Work in a group to decide how the story ends.

- How will Prince Just get Blackberry Blue away from Prince Wolf?

- What will happen to Prince Just's evil stepmother and stepbrother?

- Is there a link between Prince Wolf and the grey wolf that attacked Prince Just?

- How will Blackberry Blue's brambly cloak help her?

- Will her mother ever return to her from the bramble bush?

d Make notes about how you think the story ends and prepare a presentation on your ending of the story.

> **Writing tip**
>
> You can make notes using mind maps, tables or other planning diagrams.

2 Give your presentation.

a In your group, practise your presentation.

- Who will say what?

- Will you add storytelling effects?

- How will you add expression and engage the audience?

b Give your presentation to another group.

- Listen to each other's presentations.

- Ask questions and give feedback on the presentation and the story ending.

How are we doing?

- Did the group speak clearly and engage your interest?
- Was the story ending suitable for a fairy tale?

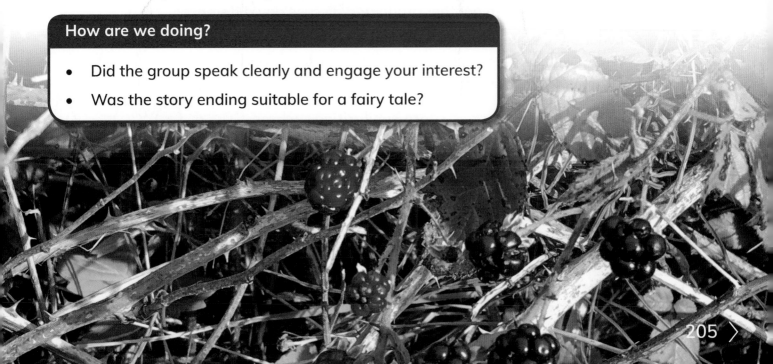

> 7.10 Compare the tales

We are going to ...

- compare two versions of a story and discuss how to adapt a story.

Getting started

1   Discuss with a partner whether or why you think *Blackberry Blue* is based on the *Cinderella* fairy tale.

2   Share your ideas with the class.

1   Is *Blackberry Blue* a *Cinderella* story?

a   Based on the extract and the story retelling, work in groups and discuss the similarities and differences between the traditional *Cinderella* story and *Blackberry Blue*. Make notes in a table.

Similarities	Differences
A prince falls in love with a mysterious girl.	

b   Share your table with another group and discuss any differences.

c   On your own, write a paragraph comparing the two stories and end by giving your opinion on which one you prefer and why. Back up your ideas with reasons.

Example: The two stories share similarities such as ... However, they are also different because ... I prefer ... because ...

2 Listen to authors talking about modernising or adapting a familiar tale.

a Listen to the audio and discuss the following questions.

- What is important to know when updating a story?
- What sort of changes should you make?
- What changes were made in *Blackberry Blue*?
- Can you think of any other changes?
- How is updating a story like the oral tradition of storytelling?

b Share in a group how you updated the Cinderella story in your synopses that you wrote in 7.5 and 7.6.

- How did you make it modern?
- What was your Cinderella character like?
- What other changes did you make?
- After reading *Blackberry Blue*, do you have any other ideas for how to update the story or make it more relevant to your region?

c Share your ideas with another group and give each other feedback.

> 7.11 and 7.12 Write your own version of a tale

We are going to ...

- **plan, write, edit and tell a *fairy story* or *traditional tale*.**

Getting started

1 Work with a partner and remind each other of the features of fairy tales.

2 Think of different ways to begin a traditional fairy tale. Share your ideas with other pairs.

1 Plan your own version of the Cinderella or another fairy tale or traditional tale of your choice.

a In groups of three, using the planning table on the next page, plan your version of the tale.

- For each part, discuss *how, why, who, what, when* and *where*.

- Decide which elements of the original story to keep and which parts to change.

- Decide whether to write in first-person or third-person narrative. Which character could tell the story from their point of view?

You could expand your synopsis or your ideas from earlier, set it in modern times or plan it in your region. Remember, the Cinderella figure doesn't have to be a girl.

Introduction	Build up	Complication	Resolution	Conclusion		
Part One Introduction	**Part Two** Build up and unexpected help or intervention	**Part Three** Climax and resolution
• Main characters? • Supporting characters? • Setting/time? • How does it begin?	• How do the main characters meet? • What does the main character want to do? • What help is given and by whom/what? • What are the conditions?	• What happens at the main event? • What is the complication or problem? • How is the problem resolved? • How does it end?

b   Decide who will write what, and write a first draft.

c   Share your drafts, give each other feedback and revise your story.
Check for:

- standard English

- traditional beginnings and endings

- different sentence types and lengths

- descriptive vocabulary, adverbial phrases and clauses, and figurative language

- different positions of phrases and clauses in longer or complex sentences

- dialogue correctly set out and punctuated

- use of pronouns and possessive adjectives to add flow

- interesting layout, text features and illustrations.

d   Use the steps in 'The writing process' in the Toolkit at the back of this book and a dictionary or your wordlist to help you check for correct spelling, grammar and punctuation.

e   Create a final version of your story.
Proofread your work and add illustrations.

2 Tales are for sharing!

a Practise reading your story aloud together, emphasising the drama and any dialogue in your delivery.

b Delight and surprise other groups by reading them your story!

Did your group read clearly, fluently and with some drama?

How could you have improved your part?

Look what I can do!

☐ I can identify key features of fairy and traditional tales.

☐ I can identify phrases and clauses, and connectives joining them.

☐ I can read a text and make predictions.

☐ I can predict how the story ends.

☐ I can adapt, write, edit and improve a *Cinderella* story

☐ I can tell our story to other groups with drama and expression.

Check your progress

1   List three features of a traditional fairy tale.

2   Identify whether the underlined words are a phrase or a clause:

   a   The prince's wicked stepmother <u>with cold eyes</u> laughed cruelly.

   b   She gave Prince Just the soup <u>that she had poisoned</u>.

   c   Prince Wolf transformed into a slavering, snarling beast <u>with sharp, glistening fangs</u>.

3   Choose the correct form of the verb to be to make these sentences happen right now.

   a   Blackberry Blue (to be) making her blackberry pies.

   b   All the girls in the land (to be) getting ready for the Summer Ball.

   c   Prince Wolf (to be) dancing with Blackberry Blue.

4   Are the underlined words adjectives or pronouns?

   a   Blackberry Blue had to leave or <u>her</u> dress would wither.

   b   Everyone stared at Blackberry Blue and wished her dress was <u>theirs</u>.

   c   She is <u>mine</u> snarled Prince Wolf as he grabbed <u>her</u> hand.

   d   <u>His</u> only hope was to follow the petals hoping they were <u>hers</u>.

5   Give three reasons why writers start new paragraphs.

Projects

Group project: find out what Cinderella is called in different regions and the variations in the tale. Prepare a poster-board project to present your research. It should contain comparative information and illustrations, and can be accompanied by music. Remember to lay out the information clearly using headings, paragraphs, tables and bullets.

Pair project: read each other's version of the Cinderella story from the final session. Then interview each other's Cinderella character to find out about the character's life and how it transformed.

Solo project: research a Cinderella story from your region. Write a synopsis of it and share it with the class.

8 > Share your views

> 8.1 Posters with purpose

We are going to ...

- **explore features of persuasive texts, compare texts and analyse a poster.**

Getting started

Consider examples of posters, shop-window advertisements or public notices. Discuss the following:

1 What do they have in common?

2 Is there any important information?

3 What kind of language do you notice?

1 Discuss the purpose of persuasive texts.

Language focus

Depending on the purpose and audience, a persuasive text aims to:

support, inform, object, advertise, sell, invite, persuade, encourage, request.

This is achieved through the layout and language of the text.

Purpose	Audience	Layout	Language
What is it for?	Who is it for?	How is it set out?	Style, tone, words?
inform, **promote**, invite, encourage	children, adults, teachers, parents	headings, sections, lists, bullets	formal, friendly, colloquial, direct

Key words

persuasive: making you want to do or believe a particular thing

inform: tell someone the facts about something

persuade: make someone do or believe something by giving them a good reason

promote: encourage people to like, buy, use, do, or support something

a   Discuss what these text types have in common.

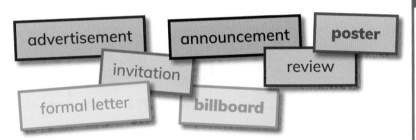

Glossary

poster: a large printed picture, photograph, or notice that you display in public

billboard: a large board used for advertising, especially by the side of a road

b   Match these purposes to the text types in question 1a.

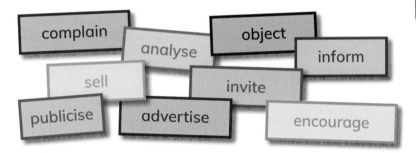

c   Explain how persuasive texts aim to:

- get the reader's attention
- persuade the reader to think, feel and act in a certain way.

d   A persuasive text presents a single point of view. True or false?

e   Summarise your discussion about the purpose of persuasive texts. Give a report to the class.

2 Analyse a poster.

BEACH CLEAN-UP

CAMPS BAY BEACH

EVERY SECOND SUNDAY 10 A.M. – 11 A.M.
WHO IS INVITED? EVERYONE
CHILDREN UNDER 13 TO BE ACCOMPANIED BY AN ADULT

WHERE TO MEET? @ CAMPS BAY BUS STOP

WHAT TO BRING? A HAT & SUNSCREEN
FREE GLOVES AND RUBBISH BINS PROVIDED

ORGANISED BY? BEACH CLEAN-UP CLUB
MEMBERSHIP FORMS AVAILABLE

a Skim the poster. Which of these text features can you spot?

Poster features

- eye-catching design/layout
- large, bold text
- easy-to-read vocabulary
- clear, direct information
- informative and inviting

Key word

analyse: to study or examine something in detail, in order to discover more about it

b   Scan for detail to understand more.

- What is the event?
- When and where is it taking place?
- Who is invited? Could you go?
- Do you have any other questions to add to the ones below?

c   Use the information gathered to analyse the poster.
    Explain the link between:

purpose   audience   layout   language

d   Add the poster to your reading log and comment on
    its purpose.

> Centuries ago, all posters
> were handmade. Posters only became
> **mass-produced** when printing techniques
> were developed in the late 1700s.

Glossary

mass-produced: produced cheaply and in large
numbers using machines in a factory

> 8.2 Layout counts

We are going to ...

- **compare the layout of texts, check the facts and identify opinions.**

Getting started

Listen to an audio describing a place to stay.

1   Which advertisement sounds more appealing?

2   Discuss which one you would choose.
    Why? What facts support your decision?

1 Read two notices and then compare the layout.

a In pairs, take turns to read each text aloud.
Which one has more expression? Why?

b Is the purpose of each text similar or different?
What is the purpose?

c How is the layout different? Which one is clear, easy-to read, eye-catching?

d What difference does the layout make to:

- the information?

- the person reading it?

e In your notebook, explain how the layout fits the purpose.
Give examples from the text.

① Accommodation in Camps Bay.

Suitable for large or small groups of family or friends.

Close to the beach with ocean views.

The rooms are fully equipped with comfortable beds, fridge, kettle, hairdryer, air conditioning and free wi-fi.

For further information or to make a booking, call Aidan on 08605123.

② **Accommodation in Camps Bay**

Suitable for **large or small** groups of family or friends.

Close to the beach with **ocean views**.

The rooms are **fully equipped** with:

- comfortable beds
- fridge, kettle and hairdryer
- air conditioning
- free Wi-Fi

For further information or to make a booking
Call Aidan on 0860 5123.

2 Focus on the facts.

a List the facts in each text. What do you notice?

b Discuss how the writer uses facts to:

- present a point of view

- persuade the reader.

c Read these sentences and identify the opinions. Rewrite them as facts only.

- Every room has spectacular ocean views.

- Our rooms are perfectly suited to meet your needs.

- The beach is only a stone's throw away. You won't get closer.

- You will enjoy your stay. You will be totally comfortable.

I could hardly see the sea from my room.

I saw only the path to the beach.

d How can you tell when a text includes the writer's opinion? What clues are there?

e In pairs, role play a conversation about going to Camps Bay to do the Camps Bay Clean-up. Take turns to convince your partner to join you. Remember to:

- include facts to inform and persuade

- use expression and sound enthusiastic

- avoid giving your opinion

How can you tell if something or someone is trying to persuade you?
How do you make your mind up about things?

› 8.3 Find your way around

> **We are going to ...**
>
> - find information, follow directions and give an explanation.

> **Getting started**
>
> 1 Talk about <u>how often</u> you use maps and timetables. <u>When</u> do you use them?
>
> 2 How are they organised to be useful and reader-friendly?

1 Explore a map and a timetable.

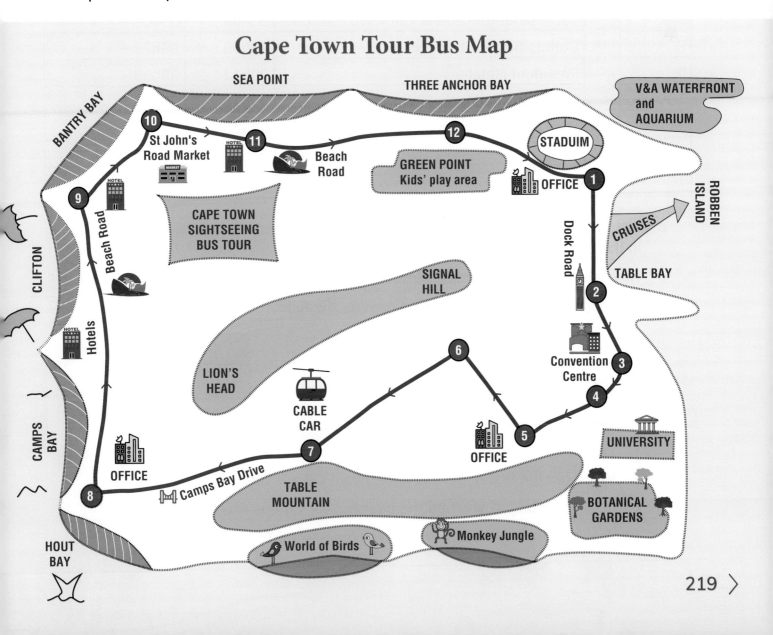

Bus Timings

Bus stop on the map	Bus stops on the city tour route	Summer Timetable	First departure	Next departure and thereafter every 20 minutes
1		Depart: V&A Waterfront (Tour office)	08h00	08h20
2		The Clocktower	08h05	08h25
3 & 4		Cape Town Convention Centre	08h10	08h30
5		81 Long Street (Tour office)	09h03	09h23
6		Jewel Africa	08h26	08h46
7		Table Mountain Lower Cableway Station	08h48	09h08
8		Camps Bay (Tour office)	09h03	09h23
9		President Hotel	09h13	09h33
10		St John's Road	09h18	09h38
11		Winchester Mansions Hotel	09h20	09h40
12		Green Point	09h24	09h44
1		Arrive: V&A Waterfront (Tour office)	09h33	09h53

a List the interesting ways used to organise and present the information in these texts.

b How does the layout and presentation help to promote this place?

c Use the map and the timetable to answer the following questions:

- Where does the bus route start and end?
- How often is there a bus?
- Where should you stop to get on an ocean cruise?
- What can you do at stop 7?
- Which stops have a tour office?
- What are the first departure times from Camps Bay?
- In which road will you find the bus stop for Camps Bay?
- List five fun activities for children to do in Cape Town.

Speaking tip

Use prepositions before a noun or pronoun to give directions.

d   Make up five of your own questions using the map and the timetable. Swap with a partner and answer each other's questions.

e   Add these texts to your reading log. Comment on why you would or would not like to take a bus trip like this one.

2   Use the map to get somewhere

a   Follow these instructions. Where do you end up? What can you do there?

> Wait outside the tour office at Stop 1.
> Get onto the bus when it arrives.
> Stay on the bus until you reach Stop 8.
> Get off the bus at the tour office.
> Cross over the road at the corner of Camps Bay Drive and Beach Road.
> Take your shoes off and have a nice day!

b   Identify the prepositions in the directions above.

c   With a partner, practise explaining how to get from one place to another on the map. Use prepositions to help you. Afterwards, write your directions in your notebook.

Example: *Depart <u>on</u> Tuesday <u>at</u> 3 p.m.; Ride <u>on</u> the bus <u>into</u> town; Get <u>off</u> the bus <u>at</u> the next stop.*

> # 8.4 and 8.5 Create a poster

We are going to ...

- plan an information poster then edit and present a final draft.

Getting started

There are many different types of posters. Name some that you have seen recently and describe what they were about. List reasons for using posters.

1 Write a rough draft.

a Pick a purpose and an audience. You could:

- tell your class about a *Pick-it-up* day around your school.

- inform the public about a *Climate Change Campaign* in your area.

- get your friends and family together for a *Walk against Waste.*

b Make a list or draw a mind map of information you want to include. Then, choose the main ideas to include in your poster. Remember to include important information about who, when, where, what, why and how.

c Consider the layout. Make sure it's easy-to-read and eye-catching.

d Choose the language and style carefully. Be direct, inviting and friendly but formal.

e Check and edit your rough draft.

Remember the following poster features:

Poster features

- eye-catching design/layout
- large, bold text
- easy-to-read vocabulary
- clear, direct information
- informative and inviting

f Proofread each other's work. Use a dictionary or on-screen tools to check the grammar, spelling and punctuation. Make corrections. Suggest ways to improve.

2 Write neatly.

a Consider the best way to present the poster. You can:

- use poster paper and write your poster with coloured poster pens
- type and print it using coloured ink
- use on-screen tools to design and display it.

b Complete and display your poster in class or in a public place.

How are we doing?

Decide how effective each poster is. What score would you give to the following features?

- purpose, audience, language, layout
- poster features
- spelling and punctuation

> 8.6 Film posters and reviews

We are going to ...

- explore film posters and reviews and understand their points of view.

Getting started

1 Do you enjoy watching films? Make a list of films you have seen recently.

2 With so many to choose from, how do you choose? What **genre** do you prefer?

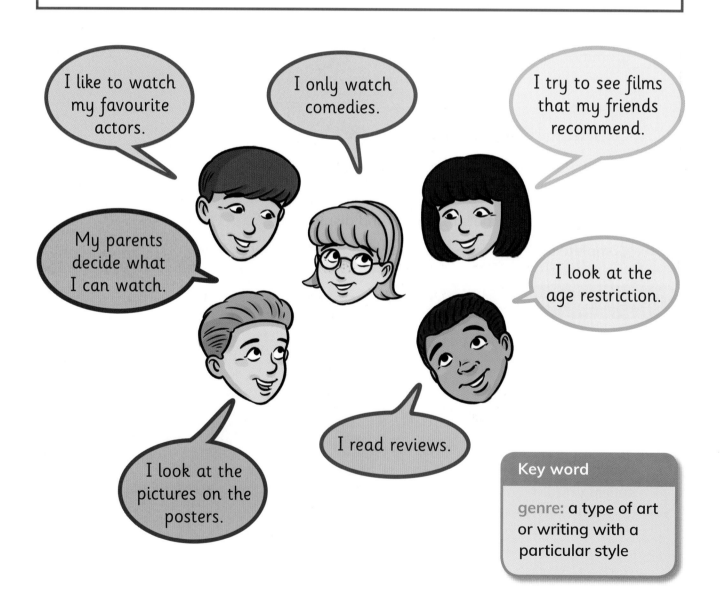

I like to watch my favourite actors.

I only watch comedies.

I try to see films that my friends recommend.

My parents decide what I can watch.

I look at the age restriction.

I look at the pictures on the posters.

I read reviews.

Key word

genre: a type of art or writing with a particular style

1   Discuss the purpose and layout of film posters.

a   Skim the film posters and identify the genre of each.

b   Which films do you think you might enjoy? Why?

c   Scan for detail. What information do these posters give? Is it easy to read?

d   Consider the layout. How does the layout fit the purpose?

e   Add film posters to your reading log and describe the genre you enjoy.

Which persuasive features influence your opinion?
Which ones don't?

2   Read film reviews and explore the features.

Hugo

Rating: ★ ★ ★ ★

Age restriction: PG

Time: 2 hours 6 minutes

Genre: Mystery and suspense

Directed by: Martin Scorsese

Written by: John Logan,
                Brian Selznick

Hugo is a touching story about the adventures of a boy who lives in a Paris railway station in 1931. The plot revolves around his **quest** to unlock a secret his father left him, while keeping out of harm's way! I had enjoyed the book so much (*The Invention of Hugo Cabret* by Brian Selznick) that I wasn't sure I would enjoy the film, but I did! I was totally **dazzled** by the magical 3D images and I thought the boy who played Hugo was the most perfect actor. The music was lively and really suited the story. I highly recommend that you see it.

Stanley Ka Dabba (Stanley's tiffin box)

Rating: ★ ★ ★ ★ ★

Age rating: Family

Time: 96 minutes

Genre: A drama about
         school and
         family life

**Written, directed and
produced by:** Amole Gupte

Set in a school in Mumbai, India, this film is about Stanley, a popular fourth-grader. His peers enjoy his keen sense of humour and his English teacher, Ms Rosie, loves his creative stories and poems. The other teachers, however, don't appreciate his talents and he's often in trouble. One of the teachers (nicknamed **Khadoos** by the children), is always after the children's lunch – greedily forcing them to share it with him. Unlike all the other children, Stanley doesn't bring a *dabba* to school. When Khadoos catches the children sharing their lunch with Stanley, he warns Stanley to either bring his own lunch or stay away! So Stanley stops going to school. This sensitive drama of friendship and belonging unfolds as Stanley's talents are finally appreciated, Khadoos is dealt with and the school principal discovers Stanley's real-life circumstances. This is a must-see film with **stellar** acting and the most beautiful music. You will find yourself laughing, crying and feeling for the children who try to help Stanley while dodging the teachers. I totally loved it and you will too.

Glossary

quest: a long search for something that is difficult to find

dazzled: if you are dazzled by someone or something, you think they are extremely good and exciting

khadoos: Hindi word for a bad-tempered, cantankerous person

dabba: Hindi word for a tiffin box or lunch box

stellar: very high-quality; excellent

Reading tip

These words are often used to express an opinion:

adverbs of degree: *very, extremely, really, too, nearly, so.*
Example: I <u>really</u> enjoyed it.

modal verbs: *should, will, ought, would, can, must.*
Example: You <u>will</u> enjoy it.

adverbs or adjectives of comparison:
Example: *She is the <u>best</u> singer.* (adjective) *She sang <u>the best</u>.* (adverb)

a   In pairs, read the reviews and find five facts about each film.

b   Identify these text features in the film reviews:

Review features

- a title and plot summary
- facts and information about the film (rating, time, genre, director, writer)
- personal opinions about the story, actors, music (the writer's point of view)
- organised into lists and paragraphs

c   Choose a review and make notes on the following:

Purpose	Audience	Layout	Language

d   Add film reviews to your reading log.
Say which film you might prefer to see and why.

› 8.7 Make film review notes

We are going to ...

- **use language for effect, summarise a film and express a point of view.**

Getting started

Use a thesaurus to find stronger synonyms for the <u>underlined</u> adjectives.

She is a <u>good</u> actor. It's a <u>nice</u> story. The plot was <u>interesting</u>.
I enjoyed the <u>lovely</u> music.

1   Use comparatives to express yourself.

Language focus

Adjectives describe or qualify nouns and pronouns.
They add interesting detail to sentences.

Notice how the words change in each form.

Adjective	Comparative	Superlative
sad scary	sadder scarier	saddest scariest
exciting	more exciting	most exciting
good	better	best

- Comparative adjectives compare two nouns.

   Example: This is a **more interesting** film than the one I saw last week.

- Superlative adjectives compare more than two nouns.

   Example: This is **the best** film I've ever seen.

- Comparative adverbs compare actions, not nouns using similar rules.

   He walked **fast** but she walked **faster** than him.

a Read the reviews again and find two superlative adjectives.

b Write these sentences using **comparative** or **superlative adjectives**.

- The first film was good but the second film was (good).

- That was the (scary) film I've ever seen.

- I was (surprised) than you when I saw what film it was.

- This film was (funny) than the other one.

- Don't you think that is the (bad) film ever?

c Identify the **comparative adverbs** in these sentences.

- The second film went on longer than the first one.

- This actor sings worse than the others.

- I like to go to the cinema more often than my brother.

d Use comparative adjectives and adverbs in two sentences of your own.

2 Summarise a film using facts and opinion.

a Choose a film you have enjoyed recently. Copy this table or make a mind map, and fill in the facts about the film using key words only.

Title	Main characters	Actors	Setting
Genre	Time	Age rating	Music
Director	Writer	Producer	Film company
Plot			
(*Don't give too much away – leave the audience wanting to know more!*)			

b   Express your opinion about the film by answering these questions.

- What did you love or like about the film?
- What didn't you like or enjoy?
- Who do you think would enjoy it? Why?
- Would you recommend it? Why?
- Was the plot interesting, predictable, exciting or disappointing?
- Was the acting convincing or could it be better?

c   What other words will help you express your opinion?

> 8.8 Present a review

We are going to ...

- **confidently present an oral review, giving facts and opinions about a film.**

Key word

oral: spoken

Getting started

1   Make a list of rules for speaking in front of an audience.
2   What do you enjoy or dislike about giving a speech?
3   Give one fact and one opinion about giving a speech.

1   Use your review notes to prepare an oral review.

a   Decide what you would like to talk about and order the information so that you give the film facts first and your opinions about it afterwards.

b   Choose key words and phrases to write on speech cards. You will use these to prompt you when you present your review.

c   Go through your speech cards. Use the review features checklist to ensure your speech is ready.

Remember to show your personal opinions by adding:

- comparative adjectives and adverbs
- modal verbs to express certainty about how you feel
- adverbs of degree.

2   Present your review with confidence.

a   Practise with a partner.
    Be aware of body language.

b   Give each other feedback and suggest ways to improve it.

c   When ready, present your oral review to the class with confidence and enthusiasm.

d   Listen to other reviews and then vote to see who would like to see the film.

Review features

- a title and plot summary
- facts and information about the film (rating, time, genre, director, writer)
- personal opinions about the story, actors, music (the writer's point of view)
- organised

Listening tip

A persuasive speaker uses tone and expression to make the information sound appealing.
As you listen, are you persuaded by *what is said* or *how it is said*?

I'd love to see that film.

I'm not keen to watch it.

It sounds interesting.

It doesn't sound like my kind of film.

How are we doing?

Watch each other present. Ask yourself the following:

- Was the presentation clear and audible?
- Was it informative?
- Was it persuasive?

Can you persuade others about something that you don't agree with?
Why might you want to do this?

> 8.9 Informal letters

We are going to ...

- explore the features of an informal letter and respond to it appropriately.

Getting started

1   How do you communicate with friends and family who live far away?
2   Do you send letters, post cards, 'thank you' notes or emails?
3   When would you send a handwritten letter?

Language focus

The language in any text has a particular **style**, **tone** and **register**.

- **Style** is the way a text is written. Style can be: formal or informal; objective or persuasive. Informal language includes slang, contractions, abbreviations and punctuation for effect.

- **Tone** is the feeling or attitude expressed by the writer. Tone can be friendly, angry, concerned or sharp.

- **Register** is about appropriate formality and word choice. Register differs depending on who is communicating with whom.

To: yashmee3@carro.com

Subject: A great idea

Hi,

I was thinking about our 'Start something' project for school.

Well, I've just had a brainwave! Why don't we start a new club – a film club! It'll be amazing! We can use a classroom one day each week and show a film after school. Obviously we'll need to ask a teacher to be on duty. Don't you think it's a great idea?

If you're keen (and I hope you are!) I'll write a letter to the principal this morning.

RSVP – ASAP!

1   Explore a text and discuss the questions.

   a   What type of text is this?

   b   Comment on the following features of the text.

      Purpose: What is the reason for the text?

      Audience: Who is it addressed to and who is it from?

      Layout: How is it set out?

      Language: What is the style, tone and register like? Is it formal or informal? Give three examples.

   c   Identify an opinion in the text. How is it persuasive?

   d   Take turns to explain how this text is different to something you write to your teacher and why it is different.

In the past, writing a letter was the only written way to communicate with friends or family living far away. It could take weeks or months to get a reply.

2   Write an informal reply.

   a   Write a short, informal text in reply to the email, using:

   • informal language

   • first-person narrative

   • personal opinion (include modal verbs, superlatives and adverbs of degree).

   b   Read each other's texts.

   • Check the text against the criteria above.

   • Check the purpose, audience, language and layout of the text.

Writing tip

Informal language often includes contractions.
You can contract modal verbs, for example:

could have = could've, would have = would've, might have = might've,
I will = I'll, will not = won't, cannot = can't, shall not = shan't

---

> 8.10 Formal letters

We are going to ...

- explore the features of a formal letter and identify persuasive techniques.

Getting started

Discuss with the class:

1 What is the purpose of a formal letter?

2 Have you ever received one?

3 Was it handwritten or typed?

4 Was it sent in the post or emailed?

1 Explore the features of a formal letter.

Name and address of the person receiving the letter

Mr T. Mitchell
Principal
Nobel Primary School
Terrace Road
Eastleigh

Sender's address and date here

Class 5B
Nobel Primary School
Eastleigh
21 November 2025

The person's correct name

Dear Mr Mitchell,

First paragraph introduces the sender and states the purpose of the letter

As part of our 'Start Something' project this year, my friend, Yashmee, and I think it would be a great idea to start a film club. We believe it will be the most popular school club. We would like to ask your permission to get it going.

Second paragraph gives further information and states the sender's point of view

We have asked around and everyone agrees that there is a need for this kind of club. Although some might think it is not educational, we think it is an excellent learning opportunity. We are prepared to do some planning and organising to get this idea to work. We will ask our teacher if we can use the classroom one afternoon each week, and if she will be on duty for us. We will also compile a list of films that the learners are most keen to watch for the teacher to approve.

Concluding paragraph sums up main points

We are very enthusiastic about our idea and we hope you are too.

Yours sincerely,
Leena Adams

Yours sincerely if addressed by name

Yours faithfully if addressed to **Sir or Madam**

a With a partner, list five features of a formal letter.

How is it set out?

What is the main idea of each paragraph?

Is there any specific wording that is used?

b Compare this letter to the informal email in Session 8.9. Copy the table and use it to make notes under each heading. Share your ideas with the class.

Purpose	Audience	Layout	Language

c Give three reasons why this letter looks and sounds different from the informal email. You can write a short paragraph or use key words to explain your reasons to your group.

2 Identify language features in the letter.

a In your notebook, write these examples from the text.

- Two facts

- An opinion (that sounds like a fact)

- A strong synonym for the adjective *keen*

- An adverb of degree

- A modal verb

- Superlative adjectives

b Does the writer express a consistent point of view?
Write a short paragraph to explain how the writer's point of view is expressed in the letter using examples from the list above.

> 8.11 and 8.12 Write a formal letter

We are going to ...

- **plan a formal letter then edit and present a final draft.**

Getting started

Take turns to explain to each other:

1   how to set out a formal letter, giving important features to include

2   what persuasive techniques you can use to convince the reader.

1   Plan a persuasive, formal letter.

a   Choose one of these ideas or come up with your own idea for a letter.

- Ask your teacher for permission to start an environmental club at school.

- Encourage the learners in your school to take part in a 'Clean-up Day'.

- Invite your peers to help start a 'Global Warming Awareness' campaign.

b   Use a mind map or table to record ideas and make notes for what to include in the letter. Decide what you will say in each paragraph. Include notes for the purpose, audience, layout and language.

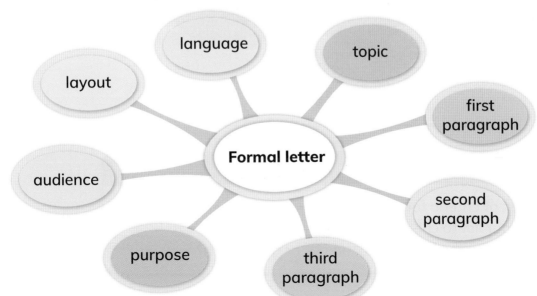

2 Write a first draft and edit it.

   a You can use the following tools to help you as you write your letter:

- a writing template or create your own
- your notes to write a first draft
- a thesaurus to find strong synonyms for adjectives and verbs
- a list of formal letter writing features
- a dictionary to help with spelling.

   b Edit your letter. Check the following:

- Have you included all the features you listed for a formal letter?
- Is your spelling and punctuation correct?
- Does is sound persuasive?

3 Write it out neatly.

   a Copy or use a writing template to ensure you follow the correct layout.

   b Choose your writing implement (a suitable pen) and check the colour of the ink.

> **Writing tip**
>
> Handwritten, formal letters should be written neatly on clean paper using a blue or black pen.

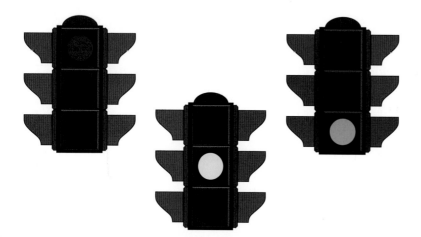

> **How are we doing?**
>
> Make a list of criteria for writing a formal, persuasive letter and use your list to check your own and other's work.
> Would you give the letter a red, amber or green card?

Look what I can do!

☐ I can recognise persuasive techniques used in different texts.

☐ I can read and use a map and a timetable.

☐ I can create an information poster to inform and persuade a specific audience.

☐ I can identify features of a film review, including facts and opinions.

☐ I can confidently present an oral review of a film.

☐ I can write a formal letter using persuasive techniques.

Check your progress

1 Describe the purpose of a persuasive text.

2 Write the superlative adjective form of:

a great

b excellent

c good.

3 Write these words in alphabetical order:

4 Show how to contract these modal verbs using correct punctuation:

a should have

b will not

c might have

5 Choose the correct words to complete these sentences:

a A preposition comes before or after a noun.

b Comparative adverbs compare verbs or nouns.

c Modal verbs describe the degree of certainty of the verb or adverb.

d A persuasive text contains facts and opinion or facts only.

Projects

Group project: make a poster about a 'Clean-up Day' at your school or local area with information on where to meet and what to bring. Include a map of the area. You can do the poster by hand or use on-screen tools.

Pair project: write a formal letter to ask permission from your teacher and/or local council to hold a 'Clean-up Day' in your school or local area. Include a description of your planned day and a reason for why it is a good idea.

Solo project: watch a film and write a film review of it. Include a summary of the plot, information on the length, actors, director and producer, and your opinion of the film and who it is suitable for.

9 ▶ Lights, camera, action ...

＞ 9.1 Predict the story

We are going to ...

- identify story genres, predict what a story is about and present your own version of one.

Getting started

Discuss different book covers of the same story, each with a different title.

1 From the book covers, predict what the story is about.

2 What can you learn about the genre, setting and characters of the story?

3 Which book would you choose? Why?

1   Discuss and compare different genres.

   a   What does it mean if you enjoy different fiction genres? Which ones do you enjoy?

   b   Make a list and discuss some typical characteristics of different genres.

   c   What genre is the story of *Aladdin*?
       Describe the characteristics of this type of story.

   d   Make a list of other stories that fit into the same category.

2   Discuss different versions of the same story.

   a   The story of *Aladdin* is very popular all over the world, with many
       versions of the same story. Have you seen the film, read the book
       or been to a live performance?

   b   What do you know about the story? Share your version of it in groups.

   c   How does your version compare with the following story summary?

ALADDIN

Aladdin is a poor **urchin** who lives on the city streets and steals to stay alive. A rich **merchant recruits** him to go into a dangerous cave and **retrieve** an oil lamp, in exchange for the promise of riches. When Aladdin realises the merchant plans to leave him in the cave, Aladdin escapes with the lamp and returns home. He and his mother decide to sell the lamp to buy food, but when she cleans the lamp she releases the Master of the Lamp! With someone to obey his every command, Aladdin's future seems bright. Until one day an old merchant arrives at his door, offering 'new lamps for old'.

Glossary

urchin: a small child, especially one who behaves badly and is dirty or untidily dressed

merchant: a person whose job is to buy and sell products in large amounts, often by trading with other countries

recruit: to persuade someone to join or work for a group or company

retrieve: to get something after first finding it

d   In pairs, come up with your own version of the story of *Aladdin*.
    Write a story summary.

e   Present it to the class.

> 9.2 Film scripts

We are going to ...

- explore a film script, identify camera angles and discuss the point of view.

Getting started

Discuss what you already know about film scripts.

1   How is a film script organised? What things does it include?

2   How is it different from a story text?

3   Would you prefer to read a script or read the book? Why?

1 Read a film script together.

a Skim the film script of *Aladdin*. What clues tell you it may be animated?

b Identify the characters and film script features in the script.

c How does the script version differ from the story of *Aladdin* that you know?

d In reading groups, choose different roles to read. Include someone to read the acting and camera directions.

e Add to your reading log. Note the differences between reading the script and reading the book.

Reading tip

Follow the stage directions in brackets to help you decide how to read your part.

The film version uses a merchant to tell the story, but the original story was narrated by the young queen, Scheherezade. I wonder why the filmmakers changed that?

ALADDIN

*(A wide-angle shot of a busy marketplace, with sellers, traders and buyers going about their business. Camera **pans** the scene then follows a merchant as he moves to a quiet doorway to whisper to the audience. Camera **zooms** in for a close-up shot.)*

Merchant: *As-salaam alaykum. Ahlan.* Greetings and welcome to you, fellow travellers to the city of Salabalabah, our city of mystique and wonder, city of wealth and fortune … for those who can find it. Come closer and let me tell you how.

(Camera zooms in on his face and follows his eyes to a small velvet bag under his cloak. Camera zooms closer as his fingers slowly release a gold string and gently remove an oil lamp. Camera moves back to his eyes.)

Merchant: *(Eyes moving from camera to hands then back to the camera.)* Do you see what I have in my hands? Yes! A 'simple' oil lamp you say – but don't be fooled. This lamp holds the secret to extraordinary things – beyond your wildest imagination. *(Camera begins to zoom away then stops.)* But wait! Let me tell you how this lamp came into my hands …

*(**Cut** to a bird's-eye view of the city. Camera zooms in on Aladdin, running away with a loaf of bread, jumping from rooftop to rooftop, balancing across a high wall and swinging down a washing line. He is being chased by a couple of guards. A high angle of Aladdin as he reaches the edge of a high wall.)*

Guard: Stop that boy – stop that thief!

Aladdin: Here we go again!

(A low angle to eye-level angle of Aladdin as he quickly checks around, takes a bite of the delicious bread, sighs with satisfaction, then takes a leap from the wall to a rooftop and continues to run away from the approaching guards.)

Guard 1: *(Low angle of guard pointing up with excitement.)* I see him – over there!

Guard 2: *(Close-up shot of his angry face.)* We have you now, you little scoundrel … freeze!

Aladdin: Freeze? But it's the middle of summer!

(Camera pans as he rushes past a group of children playing in the street. They laugh out loud and urge him along enthusiastically.)

Children: Run, Aladdin, run faster, faster, faster!

(Close up. Aladdin sneaks into a fabric shop, grabs a sheet and wraps it over his head as a disguise. He joins a group of women discussing the contents of their food baskets.)

Aladdin: Good morning ladies – mind if I sample your delicious-looking baskets today?

Woman 1: *(Laughing.)* And if we say no, Aladdin? Will you call the guards and tell on us?

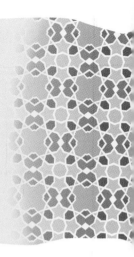

Woman 2: You seem hasty this morning ... have you got yourself into trouble again?

Aladdin: Well, you know how it is – getting into trouble is never as hard as getting out of it.

(Camera zooms in as a guard grabs Aladdin by the arm and pulls the sheet off his head.)

*(Camera zooms out quickly to a long shot of Aladdin surrounded by guards as he addresses the people watching in a **nonchalant** manner.)*

Aladdin: See what I mean?

Glossary

pan: camera action: move slowly from one side to another or up and down

zoom: camera action: move quickly towards or away from an object

cut: camera action: move the camera to a different scene

nonchalant: calm and not worried

Reading tip

The punctuation will help you to use appropriate expression and show you where to pause.

2 Explore the development of the setting and characters.

Film scripts

Film scripts include instructions for the camera because the story is told through a lens. A **cinematographer** chooses a different **camera angle** or **shot** for a **frame** depending on the purpose and message the director wants to convey about the setting or characters. The camera angle **manipulates** what the viewer sees and how they feel. It creates mood and atmosphere. Cinematographers use many different camera angles and shots to create different effects. Some basic camera angles and shots are eye level, low angle, high angle, close up, long shot and **POV**.

Glossary

cinematographer: someone who operates the camera

camera angle: the angle or position at which the camera is pointed at the subject

camera shot: the camera distance to the subject, e.g. close-up, medium or long

frame: a single shot

manipulate: to control

POV: an abbreviation for 'point of view', a shot that shows the scene from the point of view of a character

a   In pairs, add this film jargon to your wordbook so you can use it later.

b   What type of camera angles and shots are suggested in the cinematic directions?

c   Discuss what the following shots and angles tell us about the characters or setting:

| A wide-angle shot | A close-up shot | A long shot of the city |
| High angle | Eye-level angle | Aerial shot |

d   Discuss and make notes on how a point of view is expressed through a script and a lens. Then report back to the class on the following.

- What does the narrator want the audience to know about Aladdin?
- What does the writer want the audience to know about the narrator?
- How do the other characters in the scene feel about Aladdin?
- Which point of view does the audience have?

What features help you to visualise how a script will work as a film?

Does it help you to know about camera angles and shots?

> 9.3 Play scripts

We are going to …

- compare play and film script features and explore play scripts further.

Getting started

Together, discuss the following:

1   Have you acted on stage before and used a script?

2   What is the purpose of a play script? Who is it written for?

3   What features does a play script have? How does it compare to a film script?

A film script says what the audience should see. A play script says what the actors should do.

1 Read a play script together.

a Skim this play script to identify the characters in the play. Who is the narrator this time?

b How is this version different from the film script and to your version of the story?

c Choose different character roles. Include someone to read the stage directions. Read aloud. Pay attention to the stage directions to help you read with expression.

> The story of Aladdin is a story within a story because it's told by another character – Queen Scheherezade – who uses the stories to entertain the king and thus save herself.

Aladdin and the Wonderful Lamp

(*The scene changes; the street near the house of Aladdin. Music plays.*)

SCHEHEREZADE: In the street of the Clothing Makers Aladdin lived with his widowed mother, Zarita. They were very poor, and though Aladdin was a good son and loved his mother, he was very lazy. Whenever his mother looked for him, he was not to be found. He spent his days playing in the streets with other idle companions. His mother did not know what to do with him ...

(*Aladdin has appeared on the street **UR**. He looks over his shoulder cautiously.*)

MOTHER: (*Off.*) Aladdin! Aladdin! (*Enters LC.*) Where are you? Aladdin?

ALADDIN: Uh-oh. I'd better hide. I forgot to go to the market for her this morning.

MOTHER: Aladdin? Oh, that boy! He's a good son, but if only he would work once in a while! Aladdin! (*She starts off **RC**.*) Well, perhaps he's down the street. (*Going in that direction.*) Aladdin! You promised to go to the market for me!

ALADDIN: (*Watches her go.*) She'll be back in a moment. Then I'll have to go to the market. (*Sighs.*) Oh, well. (*Sighs again.*) I wish we weren't so poor. I wonder what it's like to live in a palace and wear silks and satins and count gold all day long. If I were a great lord of the city, I would ride through the streets during the day, and fling shining coins at the people. I would have feasting and dancing and singing every evening. People would come from far and wide to bring presents to me.

MOTHER:	(*Off.*) Aladdin? Aladdin! Where are you?
ALADDIN:	Over here, Mother.
MOTHER:	(*Enters DL.*) Aladdin! Where have you been?
ALADDIN:	Right here, Mother. I was waiting for you.
MOTHER:	Hmph! A likely story. You mean you were hiding from me, don't you?
ALADDIN:	Well, Mother, you see, I –
MOTHER:	Oh, never mind, son. You're a good boy –
ALADDIN:	Thank you,
MOTHER.	But a lazy boy!
ALADDIN:	Yes, Mother.
MOTHER:	Well, come along. Remember, you promised to go to the market for me today.
ALADDIN:	Yes, Mother, I remember.
MOTHER:	I finished some sewing, so we have enough gold to buy food.
ALADDIN:	Good! I'm hungry!
MOTHER:	Yes, son, I know. It seems as though you are always hungry.
ALADDIN:	We won't always be poor, Mother. I promise you!
MOTHER:	(*Sighs.*) Yes, son. Come along.
ALADDIN:	I mean it, Mother!
MOTHER:	(*Sighs.*) Yes, Aladdin. I know. (*They go off DR.*)

(*The lights come up on the Sultan's palace.*)

SCHEHEREZADE:	The Sultan of the city was a very rich and powerful man. The Sultan had a daughter, the beautiful Princess Badroulboudour. He was very fond of his daughter, and since she was his only child, he took great care that no harm would come to her. Everyone knew that someday the princess would marry a prince of much wealth and greatness. But until that time, she must spend most of her days protected by the high stone walls of the Sultan's palace ...

Michele L. Vacca and CLASSICS ON STAGE!

Key words

upstage: the back of the stage furthest from the audience

downstage: the front of the stage nearest the audience

C stands for centre

U stands for upstage

D stands for downstage

L and R stand for left and right (from the actors' point of view when facing the audience)

2   Compare a play and film script.

Language focus

A **play script** has direct speech without using linking words like *he said* or *she replied* each time. Instead, it gives the character's name, a colon and their speech without speech marks.

Stage directions are not meant to be read out. They are written in brackets, usually in italics, in the present tense.

The narrator speaks directly to the audience as a storyteller, to tell parts of the story and explain what is going on, but doesn't (usually) take part in the acted scenes.

a   Discuss the similarities and differences between a play script and a film script. Copy the table and make notes about the following features: layout, dialogue, stage directions and camera instructions.

Features	A play script	A film script
Layout		
Dialogue		
Stage directions		
Camera instructions		

b   Report back and share your ideas with the class.

c   Discuss how the setting and characters develop in films and on stage. Consider the opportunities and challenges of each. The following vocabulary will help you.

Characters: live show   costumes   make up   stunt double   dialogue

Setting: props   backdrop   set   natural lighting   location

d Use your notes to write a short paragraph explaining how film and play scripts use different techniques to develop characters and settings. Report back to the class.

How are we doing?

Listen to each other's explanations and then share and discuss further ideas.

e Add this play script to your reading log. Comment on the layout and features as compared to a film script.

> 9.4 Develop characters and setting

We are going to …

- analyse the characters and setting, and express characters' points of view.

Getting started

1 When did you last attend a live theatre performance?

2 What was it? What did you enjoy about it?

1 Answer questions about the characters and setting.

a Scan the play script in Session 9.3 to find clues to answer the following.

- Describe Aladdin's mother.
- What does Aladdin think about his mother?
- What does Aladdin's mother think about him?
- How do they feel about their situation?
- Where does this scene take place? Describe the setting.
- Who is Scheherezade? How is this character involved in the story?
- What is the name of the princess in this story? What can you tell about her?
- What does the Sultan think of the princess?

2   Change the point of view.

   a   In pairs, rewrite a short section of the script dialogue to show
       what it might sound like if:

       - Aladdin was out looking for a job but not wanting to tell his mother

       - Aladdin's mother was angry with Aladdin and cruel to him

       - they lived in the desert far from the city and the market

       - there was another character in the scene like a market seller or
         Aladdin's father.

   b   Share your script dialogue with your group. Listen and give each other feedback.

Now that you know about script writing, are you more aware
of character and setting development in films and plays?
Will this change how you watch films in future?

> 9.5 Plan a script

We are going to ...

- **compare narrative writing to scripts and plan the next scene in the story.**

Getting started

Many stories have been made into films.
Do you prefer to read the book or watch the film?
Explain your reasons to a partner.

1   Read a narrative text from the story of *Aladdin*.

   a   As you read this story extract, notice how it differs from a script.
       List the differences.

Aladdin

Aladdin approached the mouth of the cave.

It **loomed** over him like the jaws of giant beast. He heard his heart knocking and wondered if it might give him away. Down a lonely tunnel he crept. Every step took him deeper into the belly of the beast. Then he began to notice sparkles of light, little stars piercing the darkness. The light grew brighter and he moved closer with **anticipation**. The narrow tunnel opened up to show a treasure chest of jewels, gold coins and precious ornaments. How could he keep his eyes and hands off such beauty? But he must!

Then, beyond the dazzling mounds, he saw the object of his mission – the lamp. It gave off an inviting glow. With his eyes fixed on the goal, he crept closer and then reached out until his fingers could touch it. Suddenly, he felt the cave's eyes watching him and he thought he heard a **threatening** rumble from deep inside the mountain. Quickly, he grabbed the lamp clutching it tightly in his hands. As he gazed at it, he thought he saw his reflection, or something, move. With a piece of his torn trousers, he rubbed the smooth surface of the lamp and as he rubbed ...

Glossary

loomed: appeared as a large, sometimes frightening shape

anticipation: an excited feeling of waiting for something to happen

threatening: likely to cause harm to someone or something

b   In pairs, decide what happens next.

- Invent a new character to complete this scene.

- Draw a sketch of your character and make notes.

- Share your ideas with your group.

c   Use adjectives to describe Aladdin and the other character you create.

d   Decide how the characters feel about each other. Do they like each other? How do they feel about their situation and setting?

2 Plan a scene.

    a Use a storyboard to show your version of what happens next in the story.

    b Add dialogue to your story board.

1	2	3
4	5	6

    c Listen to an audio about other information you will include as part of the script called production notes.

    d Write stage production notes for this scene to add at the end of your script.

Listening tip

It's useful to write notes as you listen. Use key words only so you can keep up with writing as you listen.

How are we doing?

Check each other's planning and give ideas on how to improve.

> 9.6 Write a script

We are going to …

- write a scene for a play script, read aloud and evaluate each other's work.

Getting started

1 Take turns to explain to each other how to write a play script.

2 Make a list of criteria. Include important features to include in a play script.

3 Explain what production notes are used for.

1   Write, check and edit.

    a   Create a play script writing frame or use a template to guide your writing.

    b   Use your notes to write a first draft of the scene you planned.

    c   Check it and ask someone else to proofread it.

How am I doing?

- Does it make sense? Is it interesting and fun to read?

- Is it set out correctly?

- Is the dialogue written as direct speech without speech marks?

- Are the stage directions written in the present simple tense?

- Do the production notes provide important information about the props and stage?

---

    d   Write it out neatly or use on-screen tools to type it.

2   Perform it.

    a   In groups, take turns to read each script aloud. Take on different roles and read with expression to show how the characters might speak.

    b   Perform your reading in front of the class.

    c   Listen and respond with positive feedback and suggestions on what worked well.

Writing tip

It helps to use an editing checklist and a dictionary when you proofread your own or someone else's work. A list will remind you of all the things you need to check.

Look what I can do!

- ☐ I can predict the genre and story from the book cover.

- ☐ I can compare features of a film script, a play script and a narrative text.

- ☐ I can comment on how a point of view is expressed in films through camera angles.

- ☐ I can explain the development of characters and setting in drama.

- ☐ I can express the point of view of a character.

- ☐ I can write a new scene in a play script with stage directions.

Check your progress

1 Explain these terms and give an example of each:

camera shot

camera angle

2 Give two differences between acting on a stage and acting in a film.

3 Give two differences between a play script and a film script.

4 What are stage directions and production notes? Describe them.

5 True or false?

- In a script, the dialogue is in direct speech without any speech marks.
- There is a colon between the characters' names and the dialogue.
- Stage directions are written in the past tense.
- Stage directions are written in brackets.

Projects

Group project: choose one of your scenes from the final session. Practise performing it as a play and organise props and costumes, lighting and sound. Take different roles as characters, director and producer. Perform your play in front of a live audience or film it with a camera to replay to the class.

Pair project: research a story from another culture or land. The story must be easily adapted as a script and summarised into three or four scenes. Use a story board to explain what will happen in each scene. Write production notes with extra details to show careful planning.

Solo project: write another scene for the Aladdin script using on-screen tools if available. Your scene must include production notes and a list of characters and props needed.

> Term 1 Spelling activities

1   Letter string sounds

   a   Find a word to match each meaning and sound:

   - past tense of *buy*; rhymes with *sort*

   - difficult; rhymes with *stuff*

   - to break and turn over the earth; rhymes with *allow*

   - to make air come out of your throat with a short sound; rhymes with *off*

   - from one side of an opening or place to the other; rhymes with *clue*.

   b   - Write down the common letter string in the answer words in question 1.

   - Write down another word that rhymes with each word.

heart   beard   heard   bear   clear

   - What do you notice about the rhyming words?

2   Word roots

   a   - Find the root word for each of these job names: mountaineer, teacher, artist, engineer, charioteer, archaeologist, auctioneer.

   - Identify the suffix that has been added each time to create the job name.

   b   *Sign* comes from the French word *signe*, which comes from the Latin *signum*.

   - Look up the different meanings of *sign* and write a sentence for each meaning.

   - Think up words related to *sign*, for example: *resign*, *signal*.

   - Use each word in a sentence to show its meaning.

   c   How does your knowledge of the word's origin help you spell related words?

3   Doubling consonants

Rule: Some words double the final consonant when you add suffixes beginning with a vowel, like –ed or –ing.

If the word ends in: 1 vowel + *l, d, n, g,* or *t*	double the final consonant	*travel → travelled* *nag → nagging*
If the word ends in: 2 vowels + a consonant	don't double the final consonant	*wait → waited* *sleep → sleeping*
If the word ends in: 2 syllables with the stress on the first syllable	don't double the final consonant	*listen → listening* *happen → happening*

Discuss which words double the final consonant with –ed or –ing.

> **cool   fulfil   wait**   equal   **beg   croon** shun   **drool admit**   refer
>
> bleed   **lead**   pin   **creak   speed**   spot   **read   float**   bat

4   Adding suffixes beginning with a consonant

a   • Add these suffixes to the following words: –*ful* and –*less*.

   • Which word is the odd one out? Why?
   • Can you form a spelling rule?

b   Does your rule work when you add the suffix –ly to the following words?

busy   fortunate   steady   definite   greedy   love   lazy

c   Write a spelling rule to explain what happens when –ly is added to words ending in e.

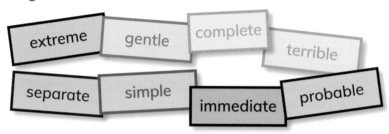

extreme   gentle   complete   terrible   separate   simple   immediate   probable

5   Exploring opposites

Opposites can be created by adding prefixes and suffixes, or the opposite can be a completely different word.

a   Talk about how these opposites have been created.

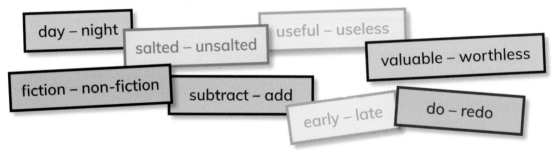

day – night   salted – unsalted   useful – useless   valuable – worthless   fiction – non-fiction   subtract – add   early – late   do – redo

b   Discuss the opposite of *light*. What do you notice?

> **Writing tip**
>
> Look carefully at the ends of the words.

> Term 2 Spelling activities

1   Silent vowel sounds and syllables

   a   Some words have a vowel sound or syllable in them that we do not pronounce when we say the word. To remember how to spell them, say each word aloud, then write it in your wordbook and underline the silent syllable.

interest	chocolate	**business**	miserable	library
different	**medicine**	memorable	**vegetable**	category
	jewellery	**deafening**	frightening	

   b   Which day of the week has a silent syllable in it?

   c   Which months of the year have silent vowel sounds and syllables in them?

2   More suffix spelling rules

   Rule: If a word ends in –y with a consonant before it, change the y to an i and then add the suffix, e.g., beauty → beautiful.

   a   Add the suffix –ness to these words:

   bossy   dozy   happy   lazy   ready

   b   Add the suffix –ful to these words:

   duty   fancy   mercy   pity   plenty

   c   Add the suffix –ed to these words:

   apply   cry   reply   spy   try

3 Plural rules and exceptions

> **Rule:** When nouns end in f or fe, change the f or fe to v before adding s or es, e.g., *half → halves.*

a   Write the plurals of these words:
    self, knife, wife, yourself, penknife, housewife.

b   Are the plurals of compound words ending in f or fe above formed any differently?

c   Find the plurals of these words: roof, cliff, chief, handkerchief, safe, chef, giraffe (clue: they are exceptions!).

4 Using prefixes to form antonyms

A prefix is a group of letters added to the front of a root word to change its meaning. Some prefixes form antonyms (words of opposite meaning).

a   Try adding these prefixes to the following words to make antonyms. Say them out loud to check which one sounds right.

> **Writing tip**
>
> Some words can be spelt either way. What about Snow White and the Seven Dwar … ?

dis   il   im   in   ir   un

> satisfied   legible   polite   credible   regular
>
> formal   relevant   probable   accurate   necessary
>
> advantage   rational   conscious   legal   visible

Check with a dictionary if you get stuck.

b   Can you find any rules to help you know which prefix to use?

c   Write a pair of sentences for six of the words and their antonyms. Use each prefix once.

d   Find two more words with each prefix and work out their root antonyms.

5   Choosing the right synonym

It is important to look at the context of the word when you choose a synonym. Not every synonym is right in a particular context.

a   Check the meaning of these synonyms and write a sentence to show how each one should be used:

carnival   event   festival   function

b   Words with a similar meaning can also differ in intensity. Order the word choices in these sentences from the least to the most intense:

- We had an unbelievable / good / amazing day at the carnival.

- The puppet show was amusing / hilarious / funny.

- The food was delicious / edible / heavenly.

6   i before e

Find a word containing ie or ei to fit these meanings:

a   someone who steals something

b   mislead someone

c   a portion of something

d   short – taking little time

e   the top of a room

f   a brother's or sister's daughter.

> ### Writing tip
>
> Put **i** before **e** except after **c** if the sound is **ee**. When the sound is not **ee**, use **ei**. When the **c** makes the sound **sh**, use **ie**. Exceptions: *seize, weird, friend, mischief.*

⟩ Term 3 Spelling activities

1 **Using that root**

a • Identify the word root or stem of these words.

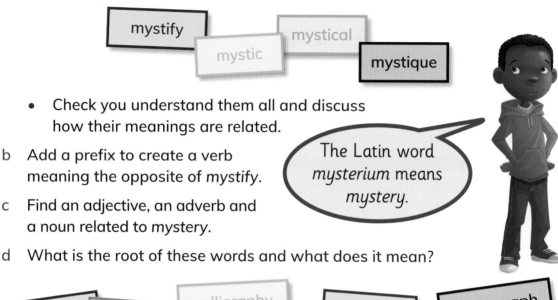

mystify

mystic

mystical

mystique

   • Check you understand them all and discuss
     how their meanings are related.

b Add a prefix to create a verb
   meaning the opposite of *mystify*.

The Latin word
mysterium means
mystery.

c Find an adjective, an adverb and
   a noun related to *mystery*.

d What is the root of these words and what does it mean?

graphite autograph calligraphy geography graphic bibliography photograph

e *Graffiti* comes from the same word root.
   How is its meaning related?

f How can knowing the root help you spell
   or understand related words?

> **Writing tip**
>
> Use a dictionary to
> check meanings and
> find words with the
> same root.

2 **Comparative spelling**

a Revise how to form comparative adjectives.

   small → smaller → smallest

   intelligent → more intelligent → most intelligent

   • How are the different methods formed?

   • When would you use each method?

b   Identify the spelling rule for these comparatives:

- large, larger, largest; rude, ruder, rudest; brave, braver, bravest

- funny, funnier, funniest; silly, sillier, silliest; bossy, bossier, bossiest

- hot, hotter, hottest; big, bigger, biggest; sad, sadder, saddest

c   Explain why these words do not follow the pattern in question 2c:

cool, cooler, coolest; sharp, sharper, sharpest; great, greater, greatest

3   Unstressed word endings

a   Lots of words have an *uh* sound at the end of them.
This sound can be spelt in lots of different ways:
er, ur, a, our, ar, or, ough, ure or *re*.

Write these words into your wordbook with the correct ending:

tract___	sup___	doll___	sof___	col___	thor___
murm___	nat___	cent___	Chin___	act___	bor___
	literat___	sew___	stell___	sulph___	

b   Lots of words end in an *ee* sound with no stress on the final syllable.
Choose the right ending for these words and write them in
your wordbook (*ee, y* or *ey*):

cit___	all___	dut___	donk___	refug___	monk___
part___	toff___	activit___	berr___	refer___	dais___
	troll___	sill___	coff___	chimn___	

4   More spelling rules for the suffix *–ing*

a   Discuss the rule for forming these present participles:

smile → smiling

freeze → freezing

shine → shining

b   Discuss the rule for forming these present participles:

try → trying

cry → crying

c   Using all the rules you have learnt, write the present participle
of each verb:

> **sleep** **think** **leave** fly sit **eat** **grind** destroy **dig** **kneel**
>
> strive spy **choose** **win** dismay

d   What are the present participles for *draw, glow, know* and *stew*?
What new rule can you write for these words?

5   Prefixes have meaning

Adding a prefix to a word does not change its spelling,
but it does change its meaning.

a   •   Add the prefix re– to these words and write the meaning of the new
word next to it.

•   What does the prefix re– mean?

b   •   Add the prefix over– to these words and write the meaning of the new
word next to it:

•   What does the prefix over– mean?

> **Writing tip**
>
> You have already learnt some rules for
> adding –ing in the Term 1 Spelling activities.

c • Add the prefix co– to these words and write the meaning of the new word next to it:

• What does the prefix co– mean?

d • Add the prefix anti– to these words and write the meaning of the new word next to it:

• What does the prefix anti– mean?

> **Writing tip**
>
> When a prefix ends in a vowel, sometimes you use a hyphen between the prefix and the root word – it makes it easier to pronounce, e.g. co-own.

› Toolkit

Parts of speech

There are eight formal parts of speech.

Nouns	Pronouns
Naming words for people, places and things:	Stand in for nouns to stop repetition
• proper nouns – names of people and places	Show possession
• common nouns – names of things	*mine yours his hers*
• abstract nouns – names of feelings and ideas that we can't see, hear or touch	*its ours theirs*
• collective nouns – names of groups of things	
Prepositions	**Verbs**
A word or group of words used directly before a noun or pronoun to show place, direction, time	Describe an action, a state of being or having something
	Different forms of a verb to show whether an action takes place in the past, present or future – the different tenses
Interjections	**Conjunctions**
Words added to a sentence to convey emotion	Connectives that link words, groups of words, sentences or paragraphs
Ouch! Oh no! Ah!	

Adverbs	Adjectives
Describe or give more information about a verb, adjective, phrase, or other adverb	Describe nouns to tell you more about them
Adverbials are groups of words (phrases and clauses) that act as adverbs	Groups of words (adjectival phrases and clauses) that act as adjectives

Not all writing needs all these features. Think about your purpose and assess what you have used. Can you do better?

Review, edit and revise

	What did I check for?
1	I followed the instructions for the activity.
2	I checked my spellings using a dictionary.
3	I read my work through for sense and flow.
4	I used a variety of sentences.
5	My sentences start in different ways.
6	My sentences make sense and are interesting and purposeful.
7	I used the correct punctuation (. , ; : ? ! " " ' ').
8	I did not repeat the same words and phrases.
9	I chose my words carefully, considering my purpose and my audience.
10	I replaced common words and phrases with more interesting ones.
11	I used a variety of descriptive words and phrases – adjectives, verbs and adverbs.
12	My sentences flow well and make sense.
13	I used simple sentences.
14	I used compound sentences.

15	I used complex sentences with different structures:
	• adverbials to start sentences, in the middle and at the end
	• subordinating connectives for different purposes (showing time, manner and place)
	• long and short forms of tenses.
16	I used tenses consistently in narrative and dialogue.
17	I used first- and third-person narrative consistently.
18	I used topic sentences, paragraphs, headings or chapters to organise my work.

Golden rules of speech-making

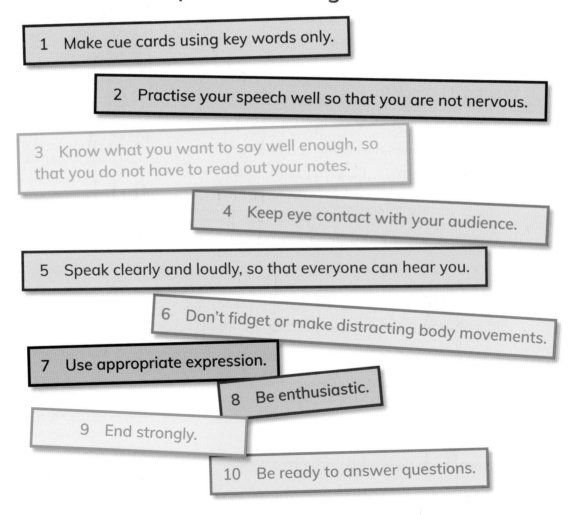

1 Make cue cards using key words only.

2 Practise your speech well so that you are not nervous.

3 Know what you want to say well enough, so that you do not have to read out your notes.

4 Keep eye contact with your audience.

5 Speak clearly and loudly, so that everyone can hear you.

6 Don't fidget or make distracting body movements.

7 Use appropriate expression.

8 Be enthusiastic.

9 End strongly.

10 Be ready to answer questions.

The writing process

Good writing doesn't just happen – you have to practise and follow a process.

Step 1: Plan

Purpose	What is its aim?	Entertain, inform, instruct, explain, persuade?
Audience	Who will read it?	Adults, children, teenagers, friends, unknown people?
Language	How formal should it be?	Formal or informal? Include slang, jargon, colloquial/idiomatic language, figurative and literal language?
Layout	How will it be organised?	What format will it have (letter, story, report, etc.)? Will it have headings, paragraphs, chapters or sections?

Step 2: Write

Write your first draft without stopping or getting distracted.
Focus on good, creative, original ideas.

- Follow the right structure and layout: story, summary, dialogue, explanation, etc.

- Use language and vocabulary to fit the style: narrative person, tense, formal/informal language, etc.

- Include details to bring your writing to life.

Step 3: Edit

Check and improve your writing.

- **Check:** Read your work. Does it make sense? Is the main idea clear? Has anything been left out? Can anything unnecessary be taken out?

- **Ask for feedback:** Can someone else spot any problems you've missed?

- **Improve:** Revise your language and vocabulary.
  Use strong verbs, descriptions and comparisons.

- **Correct:** Fix errors in your grammar, spelling and punctuation.
  Does each sentence start with a capital letter and end with a
  full stop, question mark or exclamation mark?
  Are the tenses and prepositions correct? What about the spellings?

Step 4: Present

Complete your final version with as few mistakes as possible.

- Re-read it to check for flow and final errors (use a dictionary or
  online spell checker).

- Write it out neatly in joined-up handwriting or type it out using IT.

- Illustrate or display your work creatively.

- Be ready to explain and talk about your writing to others.

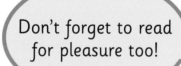

Don't forget to read for pleasure too!

Reading strategies

What you want to do	The skill to use	How to do it
Get the main idea.	Skimming	Read the text quickly to get the general idea. Focus on key words relevant to your task.
Locate specific information.	Scanning	Run your eyes quickly along the lines looking for specific key words.
Understand unfamiliar words.	Reading in context	Read the sentences before and after the unfamiliar word to help work out its meaning. Use your general knowledge to help you.
		Use a dictionary only after analysing the word in context.

Work out what's going to happen.	Predicting	Use the title and illustrations to find clues on what the text will say. Study the format and layout for further clues about the type of text you are reading.
Understand the text as a whole.	Reading closely	Use your predictions to help you read everything carefully, concentrating on the details. Read once more to check your understanding.
Write or say the main points.	Summarising	Skim paragraphs for the main idea. Explain the main idea of each paragraph in a few words of your own.
Understand what you see.	Using visual literacy	Notice important details to unlock meaning: • colours, labels, captions and other text • visual conventions, e.g. in cartoons • facial expressions, gestures and movements.
Use what you know to understand the text.	Using prior knowledge	What you already know can help you to: • understand a character's feelings • imagine a setting • understand why things happen • see how the information is useful • connect information in new ways.
Explore a text in detail to understand its deeper meaning.	Analysing	Search for underlying meaning, evidence, comparisons and contrasts in the way the text is organised and in what is said. This will help you form your own opinions and assess the content.

Researching information

Sources of information

1

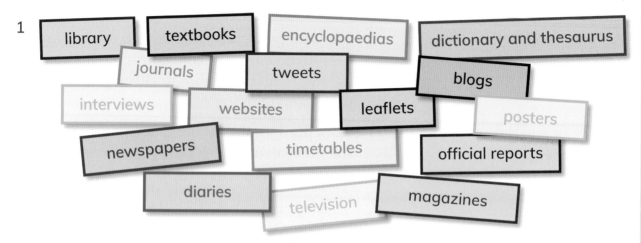

library | textbooks | encyclopaedias | dictionary and thesaurus | journals | tweets | blogs | interviews | websites | leaflets | posters | newspapers | timetables | official reports | diaries | television | magazines

2   Where would you look to find these different kinds of information?

- more interesting words

- information for a project

- what is going on in the world now

- all about another country, city or place

- family or local history

- what other people think about a topic

- how to do or make something

Online research – pros and cons

Pros

- Lots of information available

- Any topic you can think of

- More information than you'll ever need

- Very convenient

- Easy-to-use and to find information

Cons

- Can become the only source of information
- Other sources are neglected
- Little thinking involved
- Danger of copying – plagiarism
- Too much information
- Inappropriate material available
- To some, this resource is unavailable.

How to take notes on the information you've found

1. Skim the information to check it is what you need.
2. Scan the information for relevant words and details.
3. Jot down headings, key words and phrases on a mind map.
4. Summarise the information in your own words.

Writing instructions

1. Put your instructions in order.
2. Number the instructions with words or numbers: (1, 2, 3 ...,
   First, Second, Third ...)
3. Use command verbs for the main instruction (*Use, Place, Cut, Write* ...)
4. Check the instructions by making sure you could follow them.

1 Measure   2 Cut   3 Stick

Ordering your thoughts

To order an argument, you might use the following words:

1 Firstly, To begin with, Start

2 Secondly, Then, Next

3 Thirdly, Finally, In conclusion

Poet's corner

It really helps to know the jargon. You have learnt some of this before, but we've included new information too!

When we speak **literally**, we mean exactly what we say. When we speak **figuratively**, we use words imaginatively to create unusual images.

Figures of speech

Similes compare one thing to another using the words *like* or *as*. We often use them in colloquial or everyday language: *as warm as toast, as quick as lightning, like two peas in a pod.*

Metaphors compare one thing to another without using *like* or *as*. *She has a heart of gold. He is an angel.*

Personification is a type of metaphor where an object or thing is given human characteristics.

The sun glares furiously across the horizon. Shop doorways keep their mouths shut.

Sound effects are often very important in poetry – as important as the meaning.

- Alliteration is when a consonant sound is repeated at the beginning of several words for effect. *Peter Piper picked a peck of pickled pepper. Six snakes slithered stealthily.*

- Assonance is when a vowel sound is repeated. It is often used for internal rhymes. *The moon will soon rise over the dune.*

- Onomatopoeia uses words that sound like the noises being described.

The driver honked the horn. The kitten meowed piteously.

- Repetition repeats words, phrases, sounds or stanzas to create echoes or other special effects.

Rhymes appear in the middle or end of lines (often in the pattern ABCB). They can be full or half rhymes.

- Full rhymes: the final sounds correspond exactly – *flight, sight, white*, etc.

- Half rhymes: the final sounds are similar – *bold/bald, feel/spill, body/lady*.

- Internal rhymes: two or more words in a line have a full or half rhyme – *I am the <u>daughter</u> of Earth and <u>Water</u>*.

Rhythm is a sound pattern (a beat) that comes from the repetition of stressed and unstressed syllables – the way we say the words. Some poems have a set number of syllables or beats per line.

Mood is created in poetry by the sounds of words as well as the images and meaning they create. Long, soft vowel sounds help create a mysterious mood; short, harder consonant sounds create energy and urgency.

Narrative poems tell a story – they follow story conventions, but they don't have to follow the same grammatical rules as narrative text.

Synopsis of Cinderella

Cinderella lives happily until her mother dies. Her new stepmother and two stepsisters take every opportunity to be cruel to Cinderella, and when her father dies, they banish her to the kitchen to act as their servant. One day, the king invites all unmarried girls to a ball at the palace, for his son, the prince, to choose a bride. Cinderella cannot go as she has only her ragged clothes to wear.

Suddenly, her fairy godmother appears and transforms a pumpkin into a coach, mice into horses and Cinderella's rags into a beautiful gown and shoes, but she warns Cinderella to return home before the stroke of midnight or her gown will disappear. Cinderella dances all night with the prince. As she hears the clock strike midnight, she flees, dropping her tiny, glass slipper. The prince desperately searches for the owner of the slipper. Cinderella's stepmother and stepsisters try in vain to squeeze their feet into the shoe, but it fits Cinderella perfectly. She and the prince marry and live happily ever after.

Key words

> Acknowledgements

The authors and publishers acknowledge the following sources of copyright material and are grateful for the permissions granted. While every effort has been made, it has not always been possible to identify the sources of all the material used, or to trace all copyright holders. If any omissions are brought to our notice, we will be happy to include the appropriate acknowledgements on reprinting.

Unit 1: Extract from 'The Man with the cocoanuts' from *Phillipine Folk Tales* by Mabel Cook Cole (published 1916); **Unit 2:** ISRO Mission tweets from ISRO; **Unit 3:** 'The Sea' by James Reeves from the *Complete poems for Children* published by Faber and Faber Ltd. Used with the permission of David Higham Associates; An Old Silent Pond by Matsuo Basho, Translated by Harry Behn and Peter Beilenson, published in Haiku Harvest: Japanese Haiku Series IV © 1962, 2012 by Peter Pauper Press. Used with the permission (www.peterpauper.com); From 'Toward those short trees', by Masaoka Shiki. Copyright © 1998 Reprinted with permission of Columbia University Press; 'Summer sun gives, takes' by Stan Holroyd published by Hare- Yama Ryu. Offered In the spirit of the creation of haiku true to the spirit of the art form; 'Wind' from *Earth Magic* written by Dionne Brand is used by permission of Kids Can Press Ltd., Toronto. Text © 1979, 2006 Dionne Brand; 'Listen' by Telcine Turner; **Unit 4:** Extract from *The Jungle Book* adapted for stage by Stuart Paterson, published by NickHern Books; Extract from 'Why the hippo has no hair' retold by Pamela Kola in *A River of Stories: Tales and Poems from Across the Commonwealth, Natural Elements Series, Volume 4 – Fire* (compiled by Alice Curry) published by Commonwealth Education Trust. Used with the permission of East African Educational Publishers Ltd; **Unit 6:** 'Bringing the rain to Kapiti Plain' by Verna Aardema. Originally published by Penguin Putnam Books for Young Readers Reprinted by permission of Curtis Brown, Ltd; Poem 'Once the Wind' by Shake Keane in *A River of Stories* compiled by Alice Curry, illusrated by Jan Pienkowski, published by Commonwealth Education Trust Books; 'At the End of a School Day' by Wes Magee, used by permission of the author; **Unit 7:** Extract from 'Blackberry Blue' from *Blackberry Blue And other Fairy Tales* by Jamila Gavin and published by Tamarind Books, Random House UK. Used with the permission of David Higham Associates; **Unit 9:** Extract from 'Aladdin and the Wonderful Lamp' by Michele Vacca and Robert Boburka, copyright © Classics on Stage, used with kind permission. Classics on Stage has produced 24 original 'classic' play scripts, available from classicsonstage.com.

Thanks to the following for permission to reproduce images:

Cover by Pablo Gallego (Beehive Illustration) *Inside* Mats Silvan/GI; Bo/GI; David Cannon/GI; Barcroft Media/GI; afildes/GI; rudi_suardi/GI; DEA/ALBERT CEOLAN/GI; Wim van den Heever/GI; Adisak Mitrprayoon/GI; Robert Trevis-Smith/GI; PeopleImages/GI; Marlou Gaurano/GI; eye-blink/GI; Viktar/GI; Pricha Sura Vththi/GI; DircinhaSW/GI; North Wind Picture Archives/Alamy Stock Photo; Everett Collection Historical/Alamy Stock Photo; adoc-photos/GI; Image Asset Management Ltd./Alamy Stock Photo; Bettmann/GI; Photos.com/GI; The LIFE Picture Collection/Getty Images Al Fenn/GI; S_Bachstroem/GI; Keystone/GI; RIA Novosti/Alamy Stock Photo; NG Images/Alamy Stock Photo; Courtesy of NASA; Tony Ranze/GI; AFP/GI; adventtr/GI; Bettmann/GI; Sarote Impheng/GI; Compassionate Eye Foundation/Martin Barraud/GI; Westend61/GI; Encyclopaedia Britannica/GI; Viktar/GI ; Lew Robertson/GI; NASA/GI (x2); AFP/GI; Stocktrek/GI; AFP/GI; Joe McNally/GI; Pallava Bagla/GI; Alsan Alphan/GI; David Bases/GI; John Benford/Aurora Photos/GI; enter89/GI; Kaz Mori/GI; Smith Collection/Gado/GI; Joe Drivas/GI; Willoughby Owen/GI; Peter Chadwick LRPS/GI; Noppawat Tom Charoensinphon/GI; Renamon-Z/GI; mallardg500/GI; OKrasyuk/GI; Tom Pfeiffer/Volcano Discovery/GI; Coldimages/GI; David Merron Photography/GI; Martin Lisius/GI; Alastair Pollock Photography/GI; Paul Yates/GI; Khatawut Chaemchamras/GI; Peter Dazeley/GI; Cameris/GI; PictureLux/The Hollywood Archive/Alamy Stock Photo; AF archive/Alamy Stock Photo; Barcin/GI; dbencek/GI; DaveAlan/GI; JohnerImages/GI; Roman Studio/GI; Carsten Peter/ Speleoresearch & Films (x4); SinghaphanAIIB/GI; Aslan Alphan/GI; Edwin Remdberg/GI; Image by Chris Winsor/GI; schnuddel/GI; Tom Meaker/GI; photo by Pam Susemiehl/GI; Ken Thorsteinsson/GI; Pawel Toczynski/GI; davehudsonphotography/GI; Highwaystarz-Photography/GI; fergregory/GI; Diane Macdonald/GI; Helen Camacaro/GI; Pierre-Yves Babelon/GI; Blend Images – JGI Jamie Grill/GI; 'HUGO' DIRECTED BY MARTIN SCORSESE FILM COMPANY PARAMOUNT PICTURES AF archive/Alamy Stock Photo; OKJA (2017) BONG JOON HO (DIR) NETFLIX/MOVIESTORE COLLECTION LTD;/Alamy Stock Photo; 'Mulan' Mark Schiefelbein/AP/Shutterstock; METEGOL Director: JUAN JOSE CAMPANELLA. Year: 2013. Credit: 100 BARES / Album/Alamy Stoko Photo; POKEMON: THE FIRST MOVIE - MEWTWO STRIKES BACK, 1998 Allstar Picture Library Ltd./Alamy Stock Photo; Heinteh/GI; THE LION KING DIRECTED BY ROGER ALLERS & ROB MINKOFF FILM COMPANY WALT DISNEY PICTURES 1994 - AF archive/Alamy Stock Photo; Pokémon Detective Pikachu (2019) BFA / Warner Bros/Alamy Stock Photo; Flashpop/GI; whitemay/GI; ClaudioVentrella/GI; Jason Doiy/GI; Siri Stafford/GI

Key: GI= Getty Images